NEEDLEPOINT IN AMERICA

Books by Hope Hanley

NEEDLEPOINT

NEW METHODS IN NEEDLEPOINT

NEEDLEPOINT IN AMERICA

Picture of a pastoral scene, worked by Elisabeth Moody, 1735.

Hope Hanley

NEEDLEPOINT IN AMERICA

New York

CHARLES SCRIBNER'S SONS

D-2.73[MZ]

Printed in the United States of America
SBN 684-10223-4
Library of Congress Catalog Card Number 74-78283

Acknowledgments

WHILE doing research for a book one meets very interesting and wonderful people, namely museum curatorial staff and librarians. Two stalwart and by now old friends who gave me considerable help with this book are Doris Bowman of the textile division of the Smithsonian Institution and James M. O'Neill of the District of Columbia Public Library. Frankly, without their help, I don't know what I would have done.

Some new friends I would like to mention who were also of great help to me are: Linda Poole of the District of Columbia Public Library, Margaret Stearns of the Museum of the City of New York, Mrs. A. Willard Duncan, and Mildred Lanier of Colonial Williamsburg, Williamsburg, Virginia, Mrs. Elizabeth Leonard of the Cooper-Hewitt Museum, New York, Miss Madelyn Hart of the Metropolitan Museum of Art, New York, Mr. Bart Anderson of the Chester County Historical Society, West Chester, Pennsylvania, Mrs. Dassah Saulpaugh of the Brooklyn Museum, Brooklyn, New York, Mrs. Charles Montgomery of the Henry Francis du Pont Winterthur Museum, Winterthur, Delaware, Mrs. Caroline Hollingsworth Adams of the Society for the Preservation of New England Antiquities, Boston, Massachusetts, and Mrs. Luther C. Wells and Mrs. Donald S. Wilcox of the Valentine Museum, Richmond, Virginia. These names are not listed in any order, how can you compare kindness and generosity?

The following are people who also contributed to the education of an author and to whom I am most grateful: Mrs. Benjamin Ginsburg of Ginsburg and Levy, New York, Mr. Joe Kindig, Jr. of York, Pennsylvania, Mr. and Mrs. Timothy Trace of Peekskill, New York, Mrs. Elisabeth Woodburn of Booknoll Farm, Hopewell, New Jersey, and Mr. and Mrs. Richard Day of Strawberry Hill Antiques, Peterborough, New Hampshire. I would also like to mention some dear friends who assisted me in ways too numerous to mention: Mrs. Ross Thompson, Mrs. Flora Gill Jacobs, Mrs. S. Clark Woodard, Mrs. Edward Heroux, Dorothy Thomas of Yarncrafts, Ltd., Mrs. Ralph W. Nicholson and Mrs. Symes Haynes, all of Washington, and Mrs. Richard Rheutan and Mrs. J. L. Crute of Richmond, Virginia.

I am further blessed with a patient and understanding husband, interested children and a peerless editor, Elinor Parker, who edits so gracefully that you think it was your idea all along.

Contents

NEEDLEPOINT IN AMERICA

English 14th century chasuble, red velvet embroidered with silk and metal threads (Opus Anglicanum).

One

EUROPEAN ORIGINS

IN the study of the history of most things American, one must return to the Old World for origins. That is what we must do in the study of needlepoint, but a definition of needlepoint seems to be in order first. *Needlepoint is counted embroidery stitches worked with a needle over the threads of a canvas.* The best known and the simplest of these counted embroidery stitches is the half cross stitch also known as the tent stitch. The completed stitch consists of the embroidery thread covering diagonally the intersection of two canvas threads.

This definition differentiates needlepoint from other types of embroidery which are essentially free style, that is, it does not matter if the needle fails to go into a certain exact hole to complete a stitch.

The tent stitch or the half cross stitch turns up from time to time throughout the history of the civilized world, worked in different materials and called by other names but still basically the same thing, a decorative thread crossing diagonally the intersecting threads of a canvas. However, it was not always used solely for decoration, sometimes its purpose was to reinforce the material, expecially at the points of most wear.

According to Pliny the Elder in *Pliny's Natural History*, the Phrygians, an ancient people of Asia Minor, were the first to use the needle to embroider. He further states that Babylon was known for its embroideries of different colors. The Egyptians used a needle-point-like stitch to decorate their clothing over one thousand years before Christ. The Romans used the tent stitch and the cross stitch on fabrics to make them stronger and called the work Opus Pulvinarium.

Another well-known opus in embroidery is Opus Anglicanum; the English were the most skilled at this variety, hence its name. Opus Anglicanum made use of the tent stitch, but the main stitch used was the split stitch. There was much couching of gold and silk threads, the gold was actually gold wire bent and couched down with the silk. The golden age of this type of embroidery was the thirteenth century, but even before that the popes in Rome had ordered and bought the best the English could produce. One might say that Opus Anglicanum exists today as ecclesiastical embroidery. The work was done by professional embroiderers as well as nuns and great ladies.

Some of the great ladies who were noted for their needlework if not for their charming names were Saint Ethemdreda, the Abbess of Ely, who embroidered a stole and maniple in gold and precious stones; Ælfflæda, who was married to King Edward the elder in 900; the four sisters of King Athelstan; Ædgytha, the wife of Edward the Confessor, who is said to have embroidered her husband's coronation mantle; and Adelais, the wife of Henry the First.

Elsewhere in the world, Constantinople and Palermo were famous for their embroideries. In China during the twelfth and thirteenth centuries the tent stitch was used by itself. The materials used were silk on silk and the stitches were super-fine. Perhaps this is the fabled "forbidden stitch" because tent stitch was not used much in subsequent Chinese embroidery. It was forbidden because so many people went blind working it.

During the fourteenth century the usage of embroidery changed in Europe from ecclesiastic to royal. It was used for heraldic devices on clothes and horse trappings, and furnishings such as bed hangings.

The French had registered embroiderers as early as 1295. The authorities disagree on just when the London Broderers' Company was actually begun, some say 1401, all agree it was in existence in 1430. Broderers' Hall was built in 1515 in Cutter Lane, London; in

Picture (possibly a cushion cover) showing Orpheus charming animals with music. Tent stitch worked on canvas with silk and metal threads. This subject was a needlework favorite.

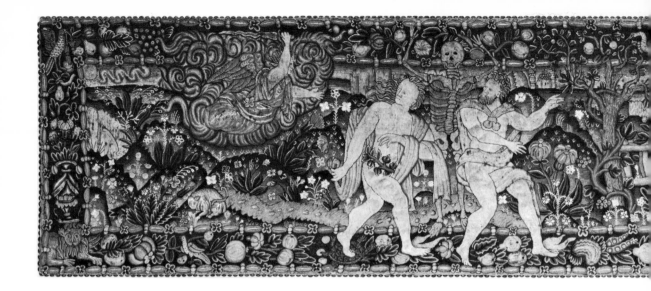

1561, three years after Elizabeth the First ascended the throne, the Guild received its charter. The purpose of the Guild was to improve the quality of work, to accredit workers and for mutual aid.

The combined forces of an increase in material comforts in the home and the great interest shown in embroidery by Henry the Eighth and later Mary, Queen of Scots, turned embroidery to more domestic and popular channels. Henry the Eighth imported embroideries from France, Flanders and Italy for his own use. The needlework done by Mary herself, and with the aid of Bess of Hardwick Hall, is famous.

It was at this time that the tent stitch really came into its own. Table rugs, cushions, bed hangings, and book bindings were made. So many cushions were worked to soften the hard wood stools used then that canvas work was known as cushions work. The cushions themselves were usually rectangular in shape and often heraldic in design. The ground was covered as much as possible to prevent wear. The corners were heavily festooned with tassels and the sides with fringe.

Some of the most beautiful canvas work ever done was worked in the sixteenth century. It has a tapestry-like quality, the shading

Bed valance depicting the expulsion of Adam and Eve from the Garden of Eden. Tent stitch in wool on canvas, from designs after woodcuts by Bernard Salomon. Scotch or English, late 16th century.

and detail is marvelous. This holds true for the French and Scottish canvas work as well as the English. This tapestry-like quality may explain why the name tapestry has been misapplied to needlepoint.

The progress of the graphic arts greatly enlarged the sources of design for the sixteenth century needleworker. Tapestries were certainly used for design ideas but with the advent of printing the embroiderer had many more ideas to choose from. Woodcut illustrations from religious and scientific books were often used as inspiration if not copied outright. One of the very first pattern books printed was Johannes Schonsperger's *Ein New Modelbuch*, printed in Zwickau in 1524. It contained patterns for the use of weavers and presumably embroiderers because some of the patterns appear to be in Holbein stitch. Other patterns are for borders and are line drawings while still others are laid out square by square on checkered paper.

Peter Quentel of Cologne published *Eyn New Kunstlich Boich* in 1527, the same year that Giovanni Antonio Tagliente of Venice produced *Essempio Di Recammi*, a lace pattern book. Often lace patterns were shown on squared paper and were used for embroidery patterns as well. Hundreds of pattern books followed from France as well as Italy and Germany through the sixteenth century. One of the best known of the French books was *Le Clef des Champs* by Jacques Lemoine de Morgue, published in 1586. It is a collection of woodcuts of hand-colored plants, birds, animals and flowers intended for the use of embroiderers, goldsmiths and tapestry-makers. It is interesting to note that Lemoine made a voyage to Florida in 1564.

England used continental books until late in the century when J. Wolfe and Edward White published *New and Singular Patternes and Workes of Linnen* in 1591. William Barley followed with *A Booke of Curious and Strange Inventions, Called the First Part of Needleworkes* in 1596. The most famous of the English pattern books are Richard Shorleyker's *A Schole-house for the Needle*, London 1624, and James Boler's *The Needle's Excellency*, London 1634. Few copies of these books exist today because of the unfortunate practice of embroiderers' pricking the designs with a needle in order to "pounce" them with powder to transfer the pattern to the material.

Herbals such as *The Herball or General Historie of Plantes Gathered by John Gerarde of London, Master of Chirurgerie*, 1636, were used extensively as pattern sources, the embroiderers using even the root systems of the plants just as shown. Thomas Moufet's (Moffet) *Insectorum*

Camel and man from Topsell's *Bestiary*.

2. Præter magnitudinem parum differt à prima, oculos habet nihilominus nigerrimos atque porrectiores antennas: ubi album colorem vides, ibi melinum sufficito, exceptis illis quasi oculis majoribus juxta finem alarum interiorum positis, quorum pupillam flammeam, semicirculum vero xerampelinum reddere oportet.

3. Non multùm colore abludit, nisi quod internarum alarum exphyses, totaque ipsarum extima lacinia glastiva sit; uti & tres illi spintheres, quos sub concava illarū parte vides depictos.

4. Omnium Regina dici potest; nam extremis alis, veluti adamantes quatuor in pala Hyacinthina radiantes, miras opulentias ostendunt, imò fere adamanti & Hyacintho oculum effodiunt. Lucent enim pulcherrimè (ut Stellæ) Scintillásque iricolores circumfundunt: his notis ita dignoscitur, ut reliquum corpus describere (licet varijs pictum coloribus) supervacaneum esset.

K 2   5. Caput

Butterflies from Moffet's *Insectorium.*

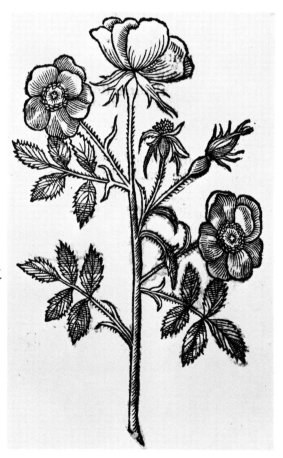

A rose from Gerarde's *Herbal.*

published in London in 1634 provided insect designs, a favorite subject at that time. If one needed animals in one's work there was Edward Topsell's work of 1607 to turn to: *The Historie of Foure Footed Beastes and Serpents.* Many of these plant and animal embroideries were worked on linen in silk, and were then cut out and applied to satin in a symmetrical arrangement. These cut-outs are called slips, obviously taken from the garden slips shown in the herbals.

Frontispiece from Vavassore's Lace Book. (*Esemplario Di Lavori*). The woman on the left of the title is working embroidery in a frame, as is the man on the right. Note the tong-type scissors in the basket at the bottom.

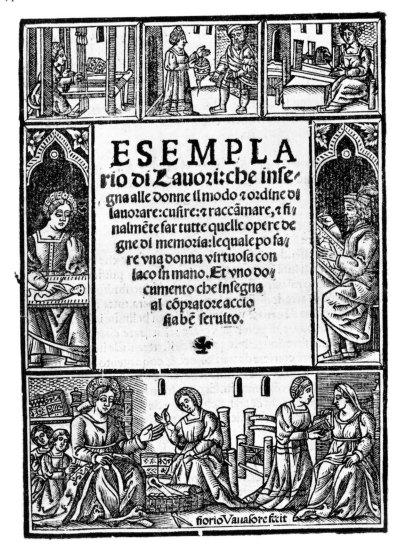

Printers of that day were thrifty men. Going to printers in other countries to buy used wood block illustrations, they would print them up on their return, making no note of their origin. It is said that some of the patterns in *The Needle's Excellency* of 1634 were copied from one of Germany's most famous pattern printers, Johann Sibmacher. Illustrations for the Bible were used from country to country in this way also.

Not all embroidery designs came from books; professional em-

Lace pattern from Vavassore. BELOW: a matchbox holder worked from the pattern.

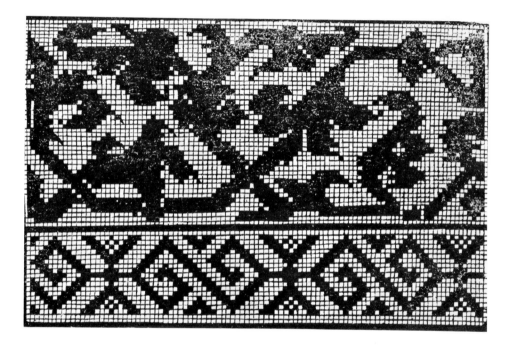

broiderers in the retinue of royal ladies were employed in designing embroidery as well as working it. John Parr was embroiderer to Queen Elizabeth the First and Edmund Harrison was embroiderer to three kings, some of his known work came up for sale in 1968. By the mid-eighteenth century professional embroidery designers were such a numerous lot that shops had ready-made designs for sale with the materials to go with them, or as we know them today, kits. The kits consisted of a fabric with a design drawn upon it and enough wool or silk to complete it.

Samplers were used as design sources in much the same way the design books were, as repositories of designs worth remembering, cloth stitch and pattern notebooks as it were. It is thought that the first samplers were lace. The earliest still existing embroidered sampler is that of Jane Bostocke made in 1598 for Alice Lee. It is in the Victoria and Albert Museum. It is a selection of geometric patterns with a few flowers and one small dog. The early embroidered samplers were done on linen for the most part, sometimes they were wide and sometimes long and narrow. The long and narrow style evidently won out as they are the most numerous. The important thing in the early samplers was the faithful recording of the design. The eighteenth century brought more emphasis on stitches and the practicing and perfecting of technique. It was then that the purpose of samplers became educational, no longer a notebook of designs. They acquired a set design and symmetrical style. You will notice that seventeenth century samplers never duplicate a motif, eighteenth century ones almost always do. The stitches used most often were the tent stitch, the cross stitch, the Queen stitch (or as we know it today, the rococo stitch) the Holbein stitch, the Gobelin stitch, the chain stitch and the eyelet stitch.

Embroidery of all kinds came into great style during Elizabeth's reign. She enjoyed doing embroidery herself and loved wearing it. It might be said that during her reign tent stitch came into being as a separate entity, not combined with other stitches or techniques but done all by itself.

Clothing was graced with the embellishments of needlework as it never had been before; gloves with gauntlet cuffs had tent stitch worked on them with fancy metal braids for trim, sweet bags, filled with sweet-smelling herbs and spices and used as we would use sachet, were usually worked entirely in tent stitch and sometimes were so beautiful that they were covered with a plainer bag. Book bindings were tent stitched, couched and jeweled, they too often had a covering bag to protect them. Until late in the eighteenth century books were

Sweet bag, English, 17th century. Silk and metal threads on canvas, the flowers worked in tent stitch, the background in plaited Gobelin stitch.

sold by the stack of pages, the binding was done to the purchaser's order. At this time booksellers began keeping books already bound in stock and soon only especially important books were custom bound.

Bed valances were worked in tent stitch on linen canvas with crewel yarns. The designs were pictorial, of biblical or mythological origin. Flowery carpets in tent stitch were sometimes used as bed coverlets. Carpets were also used as table covers and were either worked in tent stitch or in turkey work. The vogue for turkey work started in Elizabeth's time and continued into the early eighteenth century. It is a knotted stitch worked on a coarse canvas; sometimes the knots

Pair of Turkey work cushions, c. 1670.

were made as the canvas was woven. The design of the rugs was inspired by and in imitation of the imported carpets coming from the Near East. Turkey work was used as pillow covering also, the design was usually done in the turkey work knot and the background in cross stitch.

Starting in the first half of the seventeenth century, young ladies tent-stitched allegorical and biblical pictures for use on toilet boxes and letter boxes. Later in the century needlepoint pictures would be worked just for their decorative beauty, not for any practical use. Remarkable attention to detail was common to these pictures, a result no doubt of the very fine canvas used. Very realistic portraits of Charles the First and Charles the Second were often worked during their respective reigns.

During the seventeenth century the East India Company imported to England cotton hangings with a tree of life design. The design became a great favorite with textile and embroidery designers and is well known to crewel embroiderers of today. Certain elements of

"Slip" pillow with gilt braid trimming (detached needlepoint appliqué on silk).

the design were borrowed and incorporated into other designs quite foreign to the tree of life. Tent-stitchers were especially taken by the hilly or hummocky terrain out of which grew the tree of life. This feature appears in tent stitch pictorial embroidery well into the eighteenth century. The foreground as well as the background in these pictures is always very lumpy and hummocky, on each hummock there safely resides a tree or figure or animal, and most often without any regard to proportion.

The old technique of working the figure first on linen and then applying it to a satin background was re-employed in a form of needlework called stump work which was very popular in the seventeenth century. This time the faces of the figures were laid over boxwood forms or stuffed, and the bodies of the figures were padded a bit. Laces, cloaks, crowns and jewelry were then added, with a canopy projecting out over figures of royalty. The effect was truly three-dimensional. Stump work pictures were most often portrayals of royalty in full regalia and in full court. Biblical scenes were represented too, but in seventeenth century costume, two favorite themes being David and Bathsheba and Susannah and the Elders. Occasionally a confusing note was added by picturing David as King Charles, and other royal figures appeared in the other leading roles. Sometimes the faces were painted, sometimes they were worked in tent stitch or embroidered in satin. Because of the value of the gold and silver threads and jewels used for decorating the figures the pictures were usually framed, thus many survive. However, pictures were not the only item on which stump work was used, work-boxes and mirrors also survive.

Before the seventeenth century furniture was not upholstered except by loose cushions. Comfort became more of a consideration at this time. The daybed was invented, consisting of a mattress and pillow on a wooden frame with an adjustable back. Various materials were used to cover the daybeds and padded chairs, linen decorated with

Unfinished picture of Eleazer and Rebekah at the well, English, 17th century.

Stumpwork mirror frame with figures of Jael and Sisera. Note their faces, also the raised wings of the creatures in the upper corners.

tent stitch and cross stitch and hemp worked with turkey work were among them. Bargello, also known as Florentine work and flame stitch, was extremely popular.

As needlework became less of a luxury and pleasant pastime of the royal ladies, merchants' homes were graced with upholstered furniture and merchants' wives were capable of working various kinds of embroidery beautifully. New materials for new uses became a necessity. Heretofore, fine linen had been the ground for the tent and cross stitch but it was not strong enough to use for the upholstery of a chair. A coarse but evenly woven canvas was developed, the threads having very little twist to them. Some of the canvas used for upholstery then looks like a very good quality of burlap of today, and some looks like a coarse unbleached muslin. Wools were bulked up to the thickness of a knitting worsted of today, though they continued to be called crewels and sometimes worsteds until Berlin work changed the whole vocabulary in the nineteenth century.

The needlework authorities differ on the date of the first double thread canvas. One authority states that it was introduced in Queen Anne's reign (1702–1714); another says that 1820 was the time. The one-hundred-year difference is significant if one is trying to date antique needlepoint with any accuracy. This difference is compounded by the fact that any canvas that has had a stitch worked over two mesh each way will look like a two-thread canvas whether the wool wore off from hundreds of years of wear or whether it was worked five minutes ago and then picked out. Only if one can see a section of unworked canvas can one tell if it was originally one- or two-thread when woven.

An important factor in the popularization of needlework in the sixteenth and seventeenth centuries was the development and availability of the steel needle. Stone Age needles were made of bone. Needles found in Herculaneum and Pompeii were made of bronze. Other materials used over the ages have been ivory, iron, boxwood, silver and gold. All authorities agree that steel needles were first brought to Europe by the Moors and that they were made in Nuremberg as early as 1370. The Spanish, famous for their steel, made needles in quantity enough to be exporting them to England in 1597. Authorities disagree on the first English needlemaker, one story is that steel wire needles were first made by an East Indian in 1545 and that when he died his daughter married Christopher Greening, an Englishman. They settled at Long Crendon, Buckinghamshire, where Greening and Son started the first manufacture of needles in 1560. Another story has it that a Spanish Negro was the first needlemaker, and still another story claims that Elias Krause was the first. It is reported that all the men mentioned were rather secretive about the needlemaking process, thereby limiting the competition. The secret became public enough for Cromwell to incorporate the guild, the Company of Needlemakers, in 1656.

Needles were considered valuable items. Special cases were made for them, often of semi-precious stones and precious metals. In Elizabethan times needle cases resembled little scent bottles, the bottom made of quartz and the top of gold or silver. In France they were called *aiquiller* (the modern spelling is *aiguillier*) and were hung from the girdle. In the seventeenth and eighteenth centuries needle cases took many fanciful forms but were still made of precious metals. They reached their imaginative zenith in the nineteenth century when they were made to represent anything but a needle case out of such materials as wood, bone or ivory, and cardboard.

By the eighteenth century tent stitch on canvas had become thoroughly domesticated and was used anywhere that decoration was needed and a fabric would do. Wall panels in sets were used in England and pictures in frames were common. Heat screens and light screens with needlepoint decoration added a colorful touch to the drawing room. The designs used were usually floral with different kinds of flowers all attached to the same stem which twined round and round

Silver needlecase and thimble, 1739.

over a plain background. Sometimes the flowers were based in a vase. Pastoral scenes were popular and usually were set in a leafy cartouche.

Tent stitch on linen or needlepoint progressed at a parallel pace in the other countries of Europe, especially France and Holland. France's interest waned with the growth of the tapestry industry, though embroidery was still considered "the thing to do" by the royal ladies.

With the colonization of America, the emphasis of our history will turn away from Europe and concentrate on the trends and techniques of needlepoint in America. The influence of European styles and fashions were strongly felt and Europe was the main source of materials for a very long time. Fads from Europe took from five to ten years to catch on in America and some never did. The Americans adopted only what was practical at first. Fun and fancy had to wait until the nineteenth century and an abundance of materials to work with.

Prayer Book (opened to show both covers). Faith is on the left and Hope on the right, English, early 18th century.

Two

COLONIAL AMERICA

"There are few recreations more pleasing than fancy needle-work, which, while it affords ladies great opportunities of displaying their taste, makes them no less sociable to those around them. It is a graceful occupation, and an inexhaustible source of innocent and laudable employment."

The Ladies Needlework Instructor
by Mrs. Bradbee, published by the authoress
in Brighton, England, 1842

IN order to appreciate and understand the needlework of the colonists in America, one must direct one's attention to the way the early colonists lived, or survived might be a better description. The very first colonists lived in mud and wattle huts, half dug out of the earth. By 1630 with the construction of saw mills they had advanced to clapboard frame houses but with thatched roofs and wooden chimneys. Needless to say, fire was a great hazard. The home of the average colonist had but one room with possibly a loft upstairs. By the 1660's brick chimneys replaced the wooden ones, wooden shingles replaced the thatch, and if the windows were not glazed, at least they had nice tight shutters.

The walls inside were of wood planking and were sometimes daubed with whitelime. Very little furniture was shipped to the colonies with

Needlework picture made in New England c. 1785, said to be the work of Mary Woodhull who married Amos Underhill in 1774. Note the shading in the leaves. This picture is particularly charming because of the details, such as the redwing blackbird on the left, the dog about to steal some food from the basket and the fish jumping in the pond.

the first settlers, the ships were quite small and other supplies were more important, such as tools and clothing. Pegs in the walls served as closets, chests held linens and extra clothes. The bed might be a frame one set in a corner and supported on two sides by the walls and by a post on the outside corner, a very early American "built-in" bed. Tables were made of shipping crate wood. There were only one or two chairs per household, the master had the largest chair, the rest of the family made do with a backless stool or bench.

Many household necessities had to be created literally from the ground up. Looms had to be constructed from local timber, flax had to be grown from seed and then processed for weaving, sheep had to be sheared and the wool cleaned, carded and spun. The colonists imported most of their finer fabrics until well into the eighteenth century when the Stamp Act Boycotts changed their attitudes toward using English goods. The South lived somewhat more graciously because of tobacco exporting. The ships that carried the tobacco to England were larger than the New England ships in order to accommodate the great hogsheads or casks and so there was room for such things as furniture on the trip back to the Colonies.

When you consider the colonists' way of life it is amazing that any fancy needlework was done at all, the scarcity of materials and the lack of time being two major points against its accomplishment. The fact that as much of it has survived today despite the fires incidental to living in thatched roof houses with wooden chimneys is remarkable. Time, effort and no real need would be the principal reasons for the dearth of early American needlework. Not being able to afford to import special materials would probably be of less importance.

As the seventeenth century drew to a close, more colonists wrote home for furniture they had left behind and some letters specifically mention turkey work chairs. The chairs were of a straight-backed

Cromwellian style, the seat and back were slightly padded and covered with the turkey work. Possibly some of the chairs were worked in the colonies but since the materials are of European origin it is difficult to tell.

ABOVE: Chair seat, English, late 17th century, design inspired by contemporary Italian damasks.

LEFT: Turkey work chair, Cromwellian style oak frame, Dutch or English, c. 1650.

It is also difficult to prove the country of origin of some of the early samplers unless the city of origin or some patriotic motto is included, and this style did not come until the mid-eighteenth century. Known as sampleths, samcloths, saumplers and sampleres, the best known early American sampler was made by Lora Standish, daughter of Miles, about 1653 and is now in Plymouth Hall in Plymouth, Massachusetts. It is a strip sampler and consists of row upon row of flowery borders. The Fleetwood-Quincy sampler is dated 1654 and has been in the possession of the Quincy family since 1750. Its design contains human figures with three ladies at the top, then a row which includes a gentleman, a lion and another lady, with a few scattered animals and flowery borders proceeding on down the strip. Whether these samplers were started in the colonies, much less finished here, is a moot question. They may have been brought over and one can only say that they have been in America ever since their completion.

Some ethnic groups continued the use of the mother tongue in this country and occasionally one comes across a sampler in French or Swedish and later German. Unless one knows the provenance of a foreign language sampler with an early date, it is safe to assume that it is an import. There are a few clues to prove country of origin. Darning samplers are almost always English, a few were made in America but they are rare. The English took up the fad from the Dutch. The presence of crowns and coronets usually means the sampler is British. If the wool is not consistent in color or texture from motif to motif it is most likely American. The colonists were very thrifty, they used up all available scraps of wool and silk, so that you may have four different reds in as many motifs. The linen used for this type of sampler is an even weave, but coarse and tannish in color. Imported fabrics were used for best clothes, perhaps a scrap was saved for a sampler, otherwise a homespun linen would do. This is not to say all early samplers were made of scraps, but many were.

By the beginning of the eighteenth century commerce in the colonies was thriving, with many indigenous products for sale as well as imports. Captains of both American and British ships were given lists of things to buy by the colonists when they returned to England. These lists covered everything from shoe leather to items requiring tact and taste in their choice, such as a dress "suitable for a woman of forty years." Colonists returning to England bore lists of things for themselves plus a few things for speculation. Needles in "oyled papers" (to prevent rust), scissors and thread were often the subjects of such investment. They were small and therefore took up little space, and were in great demand in the colonies.

The first real commercial venture with America in such commodities was in 1603 when a group of English merchants sent a ship with trading goods to the coast of what would later be known as Maine and on down as far as the future Plymouth Harbor. The merchants hoped to trade hats, stockings and shoes as well as needles, thread, thimbles and scissors to the Indians in return for sassafras, much esteemed in that day for its curative powers.

One hundred years later more successful merchants, one hopes, than the above were advertising what was commercially available to the colonists in the needlework line, and the raw materials used for their manufacture. The *Boston News-Letter* was started in 1704, by 1706 advertisements were appearing reporting ships' arrivals, their cargoes and the location at which they would be displayed. On 20 June 1706 William Clark reported that he had just imported from the Barbadoes rum, molasses, cotton-wool, and indigo. The cotton-wool refers to raw cotton which was used for fustian which had a flax warp and loosely twisted cotton weft.

The indigo was one of the few dyes the colonists imported at that time to dye their wools, embroidery or otherwise. As early as 1650 attempts had been made to raise wild indigo in New York State by Gulian Van Rensselaer and Augustus Heerman. The French sent

RIGHT: Sampler worked by Lora, daughter of Miles Standish, dated 1653. Conventional floral designs in horizontal bands and verse.

BELOW: Sampler signed E. I., dated 1766, probably made in Pennsylvania. Note the texture of the linen.

seeds of cultivated indigo to Louisiana in 1718, where it was successfully cultivated and exported. A young lady of South Carolina is credited with changing the course of the indigo trade, her name was Eliza Lucas, later to marry Charles Pinckney of Charleston. Her father was the Governor of Antigua and because of her mother's ill health, she and her mother returned to South Carolina bringing with them indigo plants from the West Indies. The West Indies had been the source of most of the colonists' imported dyes. The first successfully cultivated West Indian indigo was raised on her land along the Wappoo Creek in 1741–1742. The business became a going enough concern for indigo to be part of her wedding dowry. Soon indigo replaced rice as the staple crop of South Carolina, which itself was replaced by cotton at the close of the century. Though the production of indigo by the Southern plantations was great, it was still considered enough of a precious commodity for it to be used by the cube as currency during the Revolution.

If real indigo were not available some colonial wives would use false indigo, but the real dyestuff was preferred. Other dyes imported were fustic (yellow) and cochineal, a scale insect whose body yielded a deep mulberry color. Madder (red) and woad (blue) were cultivated by the colonists and other colors were obtained from native plants. Sassafras yielded an orangey-yellow, pokeberry gave pink, dark olive came from black walnut bark, and black was obtained from the juice of the water hoarhound. These combined with other native plants gave the colonists quite a few colors.

In 1712 a dye house and callender-mill opened in Boston. The professional dyer dyed all colors except blues and greens until 1727 when on June first, Sam Hall advertised in the *Boston News-Letter* that he could perform such a service "which were never before perform'd in New England." He also cleaned or "scowered", stiffened buckram and made glew (sic).

An interesting sidelight on colonial needlework history is this advertisement which appeared on 1 June 1719 in the *Boston News-Letter:* "An Indian Maid about 19 years of age, brought up from a Child to all sorts of household work, can handle her Needle very well to Sew or Flower and ingenious about any work; to be Sold for reasonable Terms by James Freeman Brewer in Lyn-Street, Boston near Charlstown Ferry."

For the first quarter of the eighteenth century the advertisements ran mainly to fabrics, tapes and threads. The fabric of most interest to us is tammy cloth, mohair-like in appearance and made of wool. It was used for tent stitch embroidery as well as other embroidery uses. Balladine silk thread was offered in several advertisements, also sad (the Puritan name for the grayed hues of any color) and colored threads. Some of these items were disposed of by lottery. Linen, holland sheeting and silk thread were among the seventy-five to one hundred and fifty prizes for which three hundred to six hundred tickets were sold. The tickets went for ten to forty shillings, if you won a prize and didn't want it you could have the full price of the goods back from the dealer minus ten per cent.

Thread was considered to be of enough importance to be ransomed when stolen by pirates as shown by an advertisement in the *Boston News-Letter* of 18 June 1722. On the third of June a pirate brigantine commanded by one Low overtook the "John Hance" near Block Island and took from the adjutant of a regiment of Militias in New York various things such as a sword, a scarlet suit of clothes, a quantity of sewing silks and mohair, some dozen Jack Lancer knives, and "Sizours." The reason for running the advertisement was in hopes that anyone who had bought such goods would return them to a merchant whose address was given in New York for "a reasonable salvage."

The threads offered in the advertisements were always linen or silk until close to the end of the century when the first cotton thread spun in America was made by a woman by the name of Wilkinson in Pawtucket, Rhode Island, The Slater family of the famed Slater's Mill, also in Rhode Island, also are said to have been the first spinners of cotton thread. No cotton fabrics were made in the colonies until the last quarter of the eighteenth century.

On 3 March 1768, John Carter's store in Williamsburg advertised in the *Virginia Gazette* that yellow open canvas was for sale. An advertisement in the same paper on 28 September 1769 states that working canvas and worsted shades were to be sold at John Greenhow's store near the church in Williamsburg. These must be some of the very first mentions of needlepoint canvas in the colonies. *Dunlap's Pennsylvania Packet or the General Advertiser* ran an advertisement for Joseph Dean for 21 November 1774 to the effect that he had just imported from London, Liverpool, Bristol, and Glascow, some crewls (sic) and samplary canvas. The advertisements for crewels, crewells, cruels and worsted crewels are numerous in the colonial newspapers from the 1770's.

Silk floss for working catgut was advertised by John Carter of Williamsburg in the *Virginia Gazette* of 11 November 1773. (Catgut was a kind of open canvas used for stiffening, but evidently also used for embroidery.) One presumes the floss was an import from England though it may not have been. The Cultivation of silk was encouraged by the British from the very beginning of the colonization of America. Jamestown, Virginia, received some silkworms in 1614 to start an industry, apparently the time was not ripe though the mulberry leaves were, because the venture failed. The culture of silkworms was revived in New England in colonial times, the mulberry bushes being planted in rows and kept low so that the children could do the leaf picking. The silk was made into sewing thread.

Eliza Lucas Pinckney, of indigo fame, experimented with silk too and sent the product of her silkworm culture to England to be woven.

Chair seat, the background originally black but faded to brown; the corner is turned down to show the brilliance of the original colors, 1750.

Chair seat, with background worked in silk, the flowers in wool, American, c. 1740.

It is reported that she sent a length of the finished silk cloth to the Queen, one to Lord Chesterfield and kept one for herself.

In 1769 the British offered a bounty for the cultivation of silk in the colonies, in 1774 the importation of any tools having to do with the manufacture of linen, cotton or wool was forbidden, only wool cards were permitted. Though the colonists continued to manufacture the above fabrics for their own use with home made tools, the ban and the bounty did give an impetus to the cultivation of silk. Here was one product that did not interfer with the British manufactures. By the early nineteenth century silk was considered to have great potential for the American industrial economy, even Congress was encouraging its cultivation.

Gideon B. Smith of Baltimore imported by way of France a Philippine mulberry bush, *morus multicaulis,* in 1826. It was said to grow faster and have larger leaves than the native variety. Smith and a Dr. Pascalis of New York did such a good job of touting the virtues of the morus multicaulis that soon hundreds of thousands of dollars were being invested in cuttings. In 1835 the peak price was reached of $500 per hundred cuttings. A report was made to Congress that one acre of morus multicaulis could "sustain" enough silk worms to produce 128 pounds of silk a year worth $640. It was even suggested that worn-out tobacco fields in Virginia be turned to mulberry bushes. Even a state as far north as New Hampshire had a large cocoonery and Connecticut in one peak year produced a quarter of all silk raised. As it had been from colonial times, much of the domestic product went into sewing threads, and some was used for ribbon and men's cravats.

The bonanza ended in 1838 and 1839 as the realization came that morus multicaulis really did not thrive in the American climate, the financial panic of 1837 had already lowered the price of silk and cuttings. The coup de grace was delivered in 1844 when a fatal blight struck the mulberry bushes and almost all were destroyed.

In December of 1735 the *Boston Weekly-News Letter* carried an advertisement for John Philips who wanted New England patrons to know that among other things such as laces, gold and silver thread, lustrings and black velvet, he also had in stock at the Head of the Town Dock some needles. This is one of the first mentions of needles for sale in the colonies. A letter reprinted in the *Virginia Gazette* of 24 November 1738 from one John Ray of New York to Peter Ennis of Ireland who was planning to emigrate to America shows what a market there must have been for needles. Ray advises Ennis to bring 10,000 needles in seven sizes, as well as two hundred darning sack needles and one thousand Flemish needles. To help fill this demand further we find the following advertisement in the *Boston News-Letter* of 15 April 1742: "Needle Maker—Simon Smith, Needle maker from London, is removed from the Rainbow and Dove in Marlborough street, now in Union Street near the Corn fields, continues to make and sell all sorts of white Chapple Needles, and all other sorts round and square." Smith was one of the very first needle-makers in America, another was Jeremiah Wilkinson of Cumberland, Rhode Island, a manufacturer of hand cards (for wool). Until the time of the Revolution he made hand-drawn wire pins and needles.

The "white Chapple" needles referred to in Smith's advertisement were not a specific brand. He meant that he made needles which were similar to those made in the needle district of Whitechapel in London.

Catherine Rathall, a milliner, recently arrived from London and then residing in Fredericksburg, advertised in the *Virginia Gazette* on 18 April 1766 that she had for sale the "best needles sorted in due proportion from the finest cambrick to the largest darning needle." One can see that it was not just pioneer stock but a diverse choice. The needles that colonial ladies used were kept from harm or loss

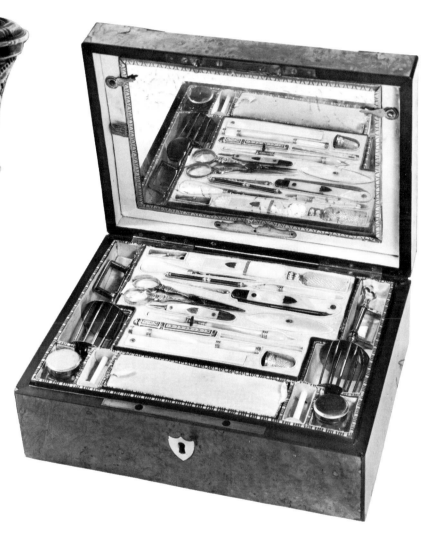

Silver thimble, powder shaker and silk bobbin. The thimble unscrews to reveal the bobbin which in turn unscrews to reveal a face patch compartment; the urn-shaped part is the powder shaker.

Sewing box with mother-of-pearl, gold and steel implements, c. 1790–1800. Initialed CVR on cover for Catherine Livingston Van Rensselaer, 1745–1810, wife of Stephen Van Rensselaer. Note the metal reels on either side of box and the cut glass scent bottle in the right back. The box also contains a punch, bodkin, lace bobbin, tambour hook and silk winders.

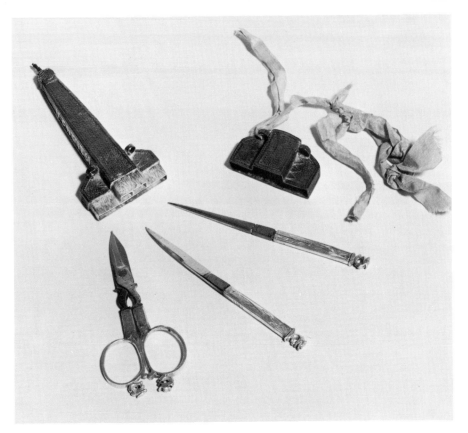

18th century covered scissors and knives, probably used for drizzling, that is, the removal of gold thread from old embroideries, a fad of the nobility in England and France.

in charming metal and ivory needle cases. Even in sewing boxes needles had their separate container matching the design on the handles of the scissors and the cap of the powder pot. The powder was used to dry the perspiration on the hands so that the needlework was not stained or the silk frazzled. In nineteenth century sewing boxes this delicate function was performed by scent or cologne kept in matching bottles, and of course containing the drying and cooling agent of alchohol. Whether a sewing box has a powder pot or a scent bottle is a general way to tell whether the box is eighteenth or nineteenth century.

The *Virginia Gazette* of 27 October 1768 gives evidence that etuis were available for sale to the colonists. Sarah Pitt informed the Williamsburg public that she had just imported "neat scissors in sheaths, superfine shaded crewels in grain, silver thimbles, morocco etwees with instruments complete, have plated or silver locks." The etuis were apt to contain, besides a nice little spoon for either beads or earwax, scissors, a needle container, a handle for crochet hooks, the hooks themselves, plus perhaps a tambour hook, a thimble and sometimes a bit of beeswax for smoothing silk.

The *Virginia Gazette* gives us one of the earliest advertisements for thimbles which were offered for sale at the store near the church in Williamsburg in October of 1751. Pins and scissors were also offered as being just in from England. It is not definitely known just who was the first thimble-maker in America, however in an article in the *Antiques* magazine of September 1967 entitled "Thimblemakers in America," Elizabeth Galbraith Sickels states that an inventory of a Boston silversmith named John Burt taken in 1746 included one

Silver thimble and thimble case with the name M. Smith on top. Note the curved top to the thimble. At right, an ivory thimble, also with curved top, and a gold band around the base.

thimble stamp. She further mentions Myer Myers of New York who in 1755 filled an order for a Philadelphia merchant for eleven thimbles.

The *Boston News-Letter* for 22 October 1767 had an advertisement to the effect that Daniel Boyer had imported from London steel top thimbles as well as thimble stamps for making them.

A sidelight on the means of payment for these precious sewing tools is shown in the advertisement of Mary Hill of Richmond on 31 October 1771 in the *Virginia Gazette*. She announced that she had just imported from London some silver thimbles and "will sell at a low advance for Money, Merchant Notes or Tobacco." A further sidelight on colonial commerce is an advertisement in the *Charleston [South Carolina] City Gazette and Daily Advertiser* on 3 February 1798 which said that Edward Blackford and Company sold enamelled and figured silver thimbles "imported" from New York.

Thimbles made before the nineteenth century usually have a rounded top. They were made from a disk of metal which was hammered into shape in a thimble stamp, or they were cut out in two pieces and were vertically seamed and then seamed again around the top. They usually lack a hallmark if made of silver, the best one can hope for is initials and a date. Horn thimbles were certainly made in the colonies and probably ivory ones. Late in the eighteenth century pinchbeck (imitation gold named after the inventor) and brass thimbles would be made, and steel tops would be included on silver ones. The nineteenth century brought squared-off tops and some time in mid-century, size numbers.

Thimbles were kept in a variety of fascinating little containers, as well as in fancy etuis and workboxes. Little silver acorns were made to hold a matching thimble, mother-of-pearl was fashioned into silk-lined eggs and chatelaines had tiny silver buckets (sometimes mistaken for the thimble itself) in which to guard one's thimble.

Before the sixteenth century scissors did not look as we know them today; two blades with loops held together with a rivet. Their shape then was more that of sugar tongs: two sharp blades opposing each other but held together by a common band of metal. They were operated by squeezing and then releasing the common band of metal. By the eighteenth century the two-piece rivetted kind were in common use, fine ones being made in England by the Sheffield and Rogers companies and also in Spain and Germany. They were often jeweled and were made of gold, silver and iron as well as steel. The blades and handles often had pierced decorations and were sometimes damascened. Early American scissors are for the most part made of dark steel of a simple but graceful design. Some look rather like Japanese flower-arranging scissors with large loops and short blades, with a slight hammered effect for decoration. Fancy scissors were made too; James Hamilton, a goldsmith from London, stated in the *Virginia Gazette* of 18 April 1766 that he made and sold pincushions and scissors in Fredericksburg, Virginia.

Chinese-style scissors, made in Connecticut, possibly late 18th century.

Persian scissors, damascene, 17th century.

Embroidery frames were never mentioned as being for sale in the eighteenth century newspapers. Presumably one went to one's cabinet-maker for such an item and he did not find it necessary to notify the public that this was something he could make. Eighteenth century floor frames were made of good hard wood, sometimes mahogany, so that warping under the tension of stretching the canvas or linen would not be a problem. Most of them still extant have nicely turned uprights and cross stretchers. Some late eighteenth century English frames have metal ratchets to adjust the angle of the frame itself. The embroidery was attached to the frame in one of two ways, the most common method was by sewing it to tapes nailed or inserted into the long bars of the frame. Some frames have a slice cut out of the long bar, the slice is hinged and covers nails set into the long bar on which to impale the tape. The vertical bars of these frames are usually of the screw type with large wooden nuts providing the tension; however, sometimes the tension was created by pegs stuck in flat vertical bars. Hand frames are similar in design, as are table frames. Table and hand frames as well as tambour or round floor frames are extremely rare. The latter most often have tripod legs and are made of light-colored woods; the hoop is often covered with tape or ribbon. Using a frame in this fashion was a common technique with canvas work. One piece of a round frame or a square wooden one would be covered with tape and then the canvas was overstitched to the frame. The Museum of the City of New York has a lovely piece of unfinished bargello work attached to a round frame in this fashion.

In eighteenth century France it was very much the style to do needlework in a frame. The French frames were much more refined pieces of furniture than ours, they often had metal ornaments of blued steel, bronze and sometimes even gold, and the woods were costly and highly carved.

The tapes used to attach embroidery to the frame were either made

LEFT: English mahogany frame, used in America. Note metal ratchets to adjust angle of work. 46 inches wide and 40 inches high in upright position, c. 1730.

BELOW: Late 18th or early 19th century frame, American. The horizontal bars have concealed nails under hinged lids, to which the canvas is attached.

LEFT: Tape loom, probably early 19th century. There are 42 spaces for the warp threads which were run through the slits as well as the little holes; the shed was formed for the shuttle by lifting and lowering the finished work. Tape made on such a loom could have been used on an embroidery frame. Commercial tape was available after 1820 and home manufacture was no longer necessary.

at home or imported from France or England. Tape was not made commercially in America until the beginning of the nineteenth century. Tapes for bonnet strings, reticules, underwear and embroidery frames were made at home on a small tape loom which could be kept in the parlor. Fine tape was made on a table loom and heavier tape on a pedestal loom. The shed for the shuttle was created by raising or lowering the finished product which was hand held.

As colonial life became easier and furnishings became less basic and more luxurious, the mistress of the house began to feel the need for a place to keep her fancy work and embroidery. In France and England exquisite little concoctions were executed in delicate woods by cabinetmakers and called sewing tables. A common characteristic

LEFT: Sewing table from the McIntyre Bedroom at Winterthur, probably late 18th century. The bag is made of silk, the inlays are satinwood.

RIGHT: Mahogany sewing table, 1790–1810. The top lifts to disclose a velvet-lined compartment with curved sectional trays at either end; underneath the trays are sections for larger articles.

of all of them is a bag-like drawer suspended between the legs of the table. Sometimes the "bags" were made of wood and then covered with pleated silk and sometimes they were just the silk lined with a sturdier material. Occasionally the bag was made of wood only and then lined with a small patterned paper. The top might have one or two drawers or perhaps a lid which lifted to show compartments in which to keep tools such as silk winders, silk reels and tape measures made to match the table.

In Boston at the turn of the eighteenth century it was the style for young ladies at their finishing schools to learn how to paint and japan on wood. One of their tasks in order to graduate was to decorate a sewing table. Some very charming American-made tables were

LEFT: Japanned work table, American, c. 1790–1810. The bag, which has been re-covered, is wood underneath.

RIGHT: New England mahogany work table, c. 1810. The "bag" is made of wood; the inlaid panels are of maple; stop-fluted legs.

embellished in this fashion. The style faded out about 1810–1815. Nineteenth century tables tended to forget the bag and enlarge the drawer space while the legs became heavier to support the added weight.

In 1642 Massachusetts passed a law that any town having more than fifty families must have a school. A twenty pound fine was levied for any town ignoring the law and some towns preferred to pay the fine rather than the teacher. Dame schools were maintained for the education of the younger boys and girls; after dame school the curriculum changed for the boys to the study of Latin and higher mathematics. Any further education a girl might acquire in the seventeenth century was at the knee of her mother. Actually her hands were needed more than her head in the time-consuming chores required for existence such as spinning, carding, basket-weaving, and just plain cooking and cleaning.

At the beginning of the eighteenth century a need was felt by some of the wealthy merchants for further education of their daughters, or perhaps they just wanted to get the young ladies closer to the social life of the cities. Mistress Mary Turfrey was one of the first to fill this need for finishing or boarding schools. She advertised in the *Boston News-Letter* in 1706 that she intended to board "Young Gentlewomen, if any Gentleman desires his Daughters should be under her education. They may please to agree with her on terms." No mention was made of the curriculum.

The first teacher to enumerate exactly what he intended to teach the young ladies was Mr. George Brownell in the *Boston News-Letter* of 2 March 1712: "At the house of Mr. George Brownell in Wings Lane, is taught Writing, Cyphering, Dancing, Treble Violin, Flute and Spinnet etc., Also English and French Quilting, Imbroidery, Florishing, Plain Work, marking in several sorts of stiches (sic) and several other works, where scholars may board."

Mr. Brownell's competition put a different emphasis on a young lady's education by listing the things he thought most important first in an advertisement on 12 April 1714 in the same newspaper:

"At the house of Mr. James Ivers, formerly called the Bowling Green House in Cambridge Street, Boston, is now set up a Boarding School, where will be taught, Florishing, Embroidery, and all sorts of Needlework, also filigrew Painting upon glass, Writing, Arithmetic and Singing Psalm Tunes."

Mr. Brownell moved his school to Philadelphia, but someone kept a school of sorts running at his old address as can be seen in this advertisement in the 20 August 1716 issue of the *Boston News-Letter*: "This is to give notice, that at the House of Mr. George Brownell; late school Master in Hanover Street, Boston, are all sorts of Millinery Works done: making up Dresses, and flowering of Muslin, making of furbelow'd scarffs, and Quilting, and cutting of Gentlewoman's Hair in the newest fashion; and also young Gentlewomen and Children taught all sorts of fine works, as Feather-work, Filegre and Painting on Glass, Embroidering a new Way, Turkey-work for Handerchiefs two ways, fine new Fashion Purses, flourishing and plainwork, and Dancing cheaper than ever was taught in Boston, Brocaded-Work for handerchiefs and short Aprons upon Muslin, artificial Flowers worked with a Needle."

A teacher in Virginia ran an advertisement in the *Virginia Gazette* of 21 March 1766 and dispensed with almost all scholarly amenities with the following: "The subscriber begs leave to inform the Public that she has taken a house in Norfolk borough, for the accommodating young Ladies as boarders; where are taught the following things, viz: Embroidery, tent work, nuns ditto, queen stitch, Irish ditto, and all kind of shading; also point, Dresden lace work, catgut, etc. Shell work, wan (sic) work, and artificial flowers. No endeavors will be wanting to complete them in any or all of the above particulars to the satisfaction of those ladies and gentlemen that may please to commit their children to the care of

Their Humble Servant

E. Gardner

N. B. She professes teaching the French Language."

A later advertisement in 1772 informs the public that E. Gardner will teach "petit point in flowers, fruit, Landscapes and Sculpture" and "also the art of making foliage, with several other embellishments

Sampler worked by Maria Lalor, New York, 1793.

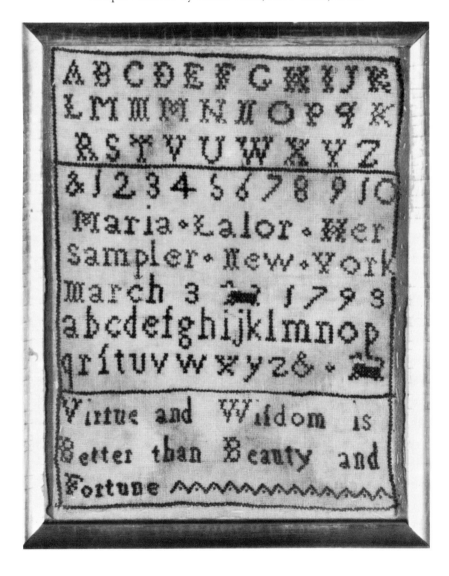

necessary for the amusement of Persons of Fortune who have Taste."

Nelly Custis, who as Mrs. Lewis was the mistress of Woodlawn Plantation, Virginia, was sent at the age of ten years to a school for young ladies in New York where she was taught sewing and embroidery by a Mrs. Graham. At fifteen she studied tambour and embroidery with the Groonbridges of Philadelphia. This was a fairly typical education for a young lady of quality. Some bright young ladies were, of course, allowed to study more challenging subjects with their brothers under a tutor , but they were the exception. The Lititz School in Lancaster, Pennsylvania, founded in 1746, was a proper academic school which also taught embroidery to its students. The West Town School, started in 1796, and the Lititz School still have a glorious collection of their early students' embroidery work. Miss Polly Balch's school in Providence, Rhode Island, was also well known for the skill of its pupils in embroidery, especially their samplers. Though the school ran from 1785 to 1831 the quality of the samplers is not as fine after 1810.

Pattern sources in colonial America were pretty much the same as European pattern sources: books, the Bible, engravings, fabrics, traditional patterns such as Florentine stitch designs, and, of course, some original designs. Mezzotint engravings were very popular on both sides of the Atlantic and many were exported to the colonies. The subject matter of the mezzotints echoes the subject matter of many of the colonial embroideries. Here is a typical list advertised in the *Boston Gazette* in 1757:

> The (12) Months
> The Seasons
> The Four Parts of the Day
> The Senses
> The (4) Elements
> The Sciences

Large floral designs were considered very appropriate for upholstery uses. Sometimes the flowers were arranged as though coming out of a vase and other times they coiled about the canvas in the style of the East Indian prints still very popular in Europe and America. Books on gardening were great inspiration to embroiderers and one of the favorites was *The Flower Garden Displayed* by Robert Furber, published in London in 1732. His floral prints had been selling well before that date in the form of a catalogue called "The Twelve Months of Flowers." In his prints each flower is identified by a number which corresponds to a legend at the bottom of the print. The flowers are arranged in gray bas-relief vases and about thirty-two different flowers are shown in each print. The flowers were apt to be very much the same in America as in Europe since seeds were a big export item both for agricultural endeavors as well as a little touch of home. One wonders when one looks at colonial needlework if one is admiring some of the floral favorites such as venus navelwort, princess feather, sweet feabus, catch-fly and Queen Margarets. More familiar favorites were the carnation, hollyhock and centaurea cyanus also known as bachelor's button.

Pattern drawing became a profession in England in the eighteenth century and it appears from the following advertisement in the *Boston Gazette* for 26 September to 3 October 1737 that there was at least one practitioner of the art in the colonies: "All sorts of Drawing for Embroidery, Childrens quilted Peaks, drawn or work'd, caps set for Women and Children; or any sort of Needle Work done by Mrs. Mary Sewall, Widow, near the Orange Tree."

Not all the patterns were custom work as is shown in this advertisement from the *Boston News-Letter* of 27 April 1738: "To be had at Mrs. Condy's near The Old North Meeting House, all sorts of beautiful figures on Canvas, for Tent Stick; the Patterns from London, but drawn by her much cheaper than English drawing; all sorts of Canvas, without drawing, also silk shades, slacks, Floss, Cruells of all Sorts, the best White Chapel Needles, and every thing for all Sorts of Work." This is the same Mrs. Susannah Condy who had a shop and boarding school and to whom is attributed the "Fishing Lady" patterns. As a result of research done by Mrs. Nancy Graves Cabot, close to sixty-five of these tent stitch on linen pictures have been traced, all worked around the middle of the eighteenth century. Present in all the pastoral scenes is a lady sitting by a stream with a fishing pole, hence the name; it is thought that she is fishing at Boston Common. Also present in the pictures is a variety of sheep, dogs, birds, deer and ladies and gentlemen. The gentlemen often have silver lace buttons on their coats, the fauna look at one with shiny beady eyes, and sometimes the people will have black beads for eyes too. The sheep have fleecy French knotted coats. Crewels, silks and metal threads were used. The pictures sometimes measure as long as three or four feet, the drawing is rather crude in style and the proportions are quite distorted but the effect is quite delightful.

Artists of a more general nature also did some pattern work for embroidery as shown by this advertisement in the *Boston Gazette* of 18 December 1758: "Japanning—This is to inform the Public, that David Mason, Japanner has open'd a shop under Messieurs Edes and Gill's Printing Office where all Sorts of Painting, Japanning, Gilding and Varnishing are done. Coats of Arms, Drawings on Sattin or Canvis for Embroidering; also pictures framed after the neatest manner."

PAGE 56. Picture, tent stitch on linen, dated 1749. Some details have been copied from the engraving opposite.

PAGE 57. Engraving from John Baskerville's *Virgil,* printed in Birmingham, England, originally done by W. Hollar after the work of F. Cleyn and first published in Ogilby's *Virgil,* 1654. This engraving illustrates *Georgic I.*

F. Clein inu. W. Hollar fecit

A "Fishing Lady" picture, tent stitch on linen; she is in the center of the picture. Made by Sarah Warren, 1741. Note the candle holders on either side.

If one lived too far from a needlework shop or teacher one pressed into service anyone with the slightest artistic ability. An entry in the journal of Philip Vickers Fithian, a private teacher at a plantation in Virginia in 1773, reads: "Spent most of the Day at the great House hearing the various Instruments of Music. Evening, at Miss Prissy's Request I drew for her some Flowers on Linen which she is going to imbroider, for a various Counterpane."

Had Miss Prissy so wanted, she could have sent to Williamsburg to Dixon and Hunter, the publishers at that time of the *Virginia Gazette*, who had a list of books for sale in January of 1777, also Ivory, Ebony or Horn pounce boxes, with which she could have copied an engraving. To do this, holes were pricked around the outlines of pictures and then the pounces full of powder or charcoal were

RIGHT: Queen Anne style side chair, c. 1730, of American walnut. The needlework is in the style of *The Flower Garden Displayed* by Robert Furber.

BELOW, LEFT: Wing chair upholstered in flame stitch in a variation of the carnation pattern, Philadelphia, 1740–1750.

BELOW, RIGHT: Miniature pole screen, mahogany; American, 18th century. Height $21\frac{1}{2}$ inches. Adjustable panel of point d'Hongrie or bargello in shaded reds, blues, tan, brown and ivory wools on linen canvas.

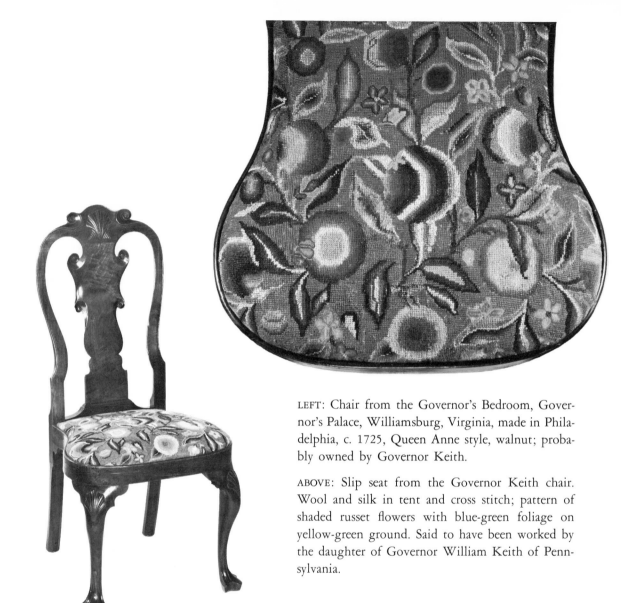

LEFT: Chair from the Governor's Bedroom, Governor's Palace, Williamsburg, Virginia, made in Philadelphia, c. 1725, Queen Anne style, walnut; probably owned by Governor Keith.

ABOVE: Slip seat from the Governor Keith chair. Wool and silk in tent and cross stitch; pattern of shaded russet flowers with blue-green foliage on yellow-green ground. Said to have been worked by the daughter of Governor William Keith of Pennsylvania.

used to sift through the holes and leave the pattern on the fabric underneath. The outline was then drawn in from the powdery trail. Colors were never indicated, one knew how to shade as part of one's needlework education. Some eighteenth century samplers and needle-

RIGHT: Side chair, New York, c. 1775.

ABOVE: Slip seat from the same chair. The needle-point is said to have been worked by Elizabeth Bancker before her marriage to General Samuel Blachley Webb in 1779.

work pictures have round or oval areas that seem to be padded almost like stump work. These areas, on examination at the back of the work, usually have been worked in the tent stitch circularly and rather tightly. That is, the work has been started in the center of the area

LEFT: Queen Anne style armchair, Philadelphia, c. 1740–1750.

ABOVE: Slip seat of the chair at left, showing a milk-maid and a huntsman framed by a border of flowers. Note the rabbit slung over the huntsman's shoulder and the bee with stinger in the lower left corner.

and then worked round and round, rather than in rows. Sometimes the eighteenth century ladies followed the curve of a leaf or petal with their stitches, rather than the straight rows of mesh in that particular space; this was done most often when shading was involved,

RIGHT: 18th century Bible, needlepoint cover.

BELOW: Tent stitch purse, wool on linen, 18th century.

BELOW: Chair seat worked by Ann Marsh of Chester County, Pennsylvania, an ardent needlewoman and needlework teacher; she came to this country in 1737, lived in Wollistown, Pennsylvania, and died in 1797. Many examples of her work are preserved in the Chester County Historical Society. This seat is worked in tent stitch with the flower stamens in French knots.

and one suspects that is the reason for it, to shade as one went along as one would do with a paint brush rather than a needle. The shading of the finished product showed one's taste and skill. All of this was to change with the turn of the century, since with the advent of printed patterns one's personal opinion would not be required when each color was already carefully marked out for each and every stitch.

LEFT: Pincushion worked in cross stitch, marked H. P., 1746.

RIGHT: Man's wallet, with tapes for closing it, worked in bargello stitch, 1768. Typical colors were red, yellow and green, with some white and blue.

Three

THE BERLIN PERIOD

THE HUSBAND'S COMPLAINT

I hate the name of German wool
In all its colours bright
Of chairs and stools in fancy work
I hate the very sight!
The rugs and slippers that I've seen,
The ottomans and bags
Sooner than wear a stitch on me
I'd walk the street in rags.

Oh, Heaven preserve me from a wife
With "fancy work" run wild
And hands which never do aught else
For husband or for child.
Our clothes are rent, our bills unpaid,
Our house is in disorder,
AND ALL BECAUSE MY LADY-WIFE
HAS TAKEN TO EMBROIDER!

From *British and American Tapestries*
by Mary Eirwen Jones
Tower Bridge Publications England, 1952

THE nineteenth century brought a marked change to the general style of needlepoint. Ladies would rely less and less on their own artistry or a "custom" drawn pattern, fewer ladies would exercise their own choice in the colors they used. This was the century of following the fad, doing what was stylish in home decoration as well as needle-work. The trend had started the century before with a craze for beaded and knit purses. White work was also very much the thing to do as was silk embroidery on satin ground. The interest shown in these forms of needlework was infinitesimal when compared with that

65

shown the "rage" that was to come, called Berlin Work. The rage lasted for over half a century and in itself created an industry.

The last century had seen needlepoint patterns marked off on graph or checkered paper but only in black and white and with no colors indicated. Pattern books such as *Das Neuen Strick-Buchlein* published in the late eighteenth century in Nurnberg by Christoph Weigel, Junior, contained damask-like patterns with crowns and flowers marked out on graph paper. Two alphabets were included. These designs, marked by a little star-like symbol in each pattern square were intended for knitting, but a caption notes that they may be used for embroidery too.

In 1802 John Frederic Netto, a landscape painter and engraving copier, had published in Leipzig a set of knitting pattern plates in book form entitled *L'Art de Tricoter*. The pattern is shown by a dot in the squares of the engraved and checkered plate; they are mostly floral patterns. Each plate is reproduced twice, once with just the dots in black to show the pattern, and the second time with the colors painted over the dots, but in a free style, not filling each square.

Surely some clever young lady had colored in the patterns she worked to make it easier to remember the colors and their arrangement before Netto produced his book, but it remained for another landscape painter and engraving copier named A. Philipson to see the commercial aspects of colored needlework patterns. In order to make coloring easier for the artists (it was all done by hand) he engraved different little symbols for each color on the outside outline of each object in the pattern. There would be no tedious checking of the master copy for each little square, just "paint by the symbols" so to speak. Further, he filled in the color of each square completely, not free hand as Netto had done. The earliest known and still existing example of his patterns are in a little book he had published in Berlin in 1803. It contains fourteen plates of Blumen, Bouquets, Guirlanden,

Detail from an 18th century knitting pattern
book published by Christoph Weigel, Jr.

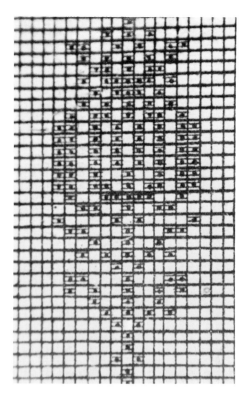

Detail from A. Phillipson book,
published in 1803.

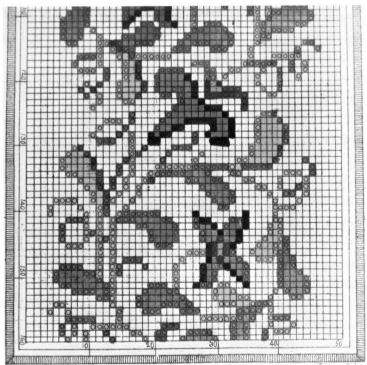

Pattern of three children in a garden, published by L. W. Wittich, Berlin.

Rosetten, Arabesken, Vasen and Landschaften. In the foreword Philipson mentions another book previously published by him that was so well received he decided to follow up his success by getting together this publication and he promises a third. He further states that each square means a stitch but he does not specify just what kind of a stitch. The patterns consist of borders of flowers and leaves, geometric repeat patterns and two landscapes, a castle and a Roman temple. The colors in some of the patterns are quite pleasing, in others quite garish, for instance, the combination of two shades of orange plus black and purple.

We next hear of Philipson with the publication in Leipzig of a ladies' yearbook, as they were sometimes called. He had two pages of needlepoint patterns in the *Zweites Toiletten-Gelchent Lin Fahrbuch Fur Damen* published by Georg Vos in 1806. These yearbooks were like ladies' magazines but produced on a much grander scale. They contained classic engravings, little songs, poems and essays, as well as exercise instructions, white work patterns, knitting patterns for reticules and instructions for making flowers from silk, plus embroidery patterns on checkered or "point" paper. Philipson's patterns again have the symbols for the artists, the colors are bright and the subjects are floral borders, geometric repeats and another castle, this time on its own island. Netto did most of the other illustrations in this yearbook.

Evidently Philipson's idea was well thought of because he soon had competition. L. W. Wittich of Berlin started to produce patterns in color around 1810, according to the Countess of Wilton's book, *The Art of Needlework*. Frau Wittich is mentioned as being the driving force in the continued production of patterns, though the initials L. W. are probably Herr Wittich's. The Wittich enterprise added a new facet to the business by having trained artists, called mustermaler, copy famous paintings and then reduce them to the squares

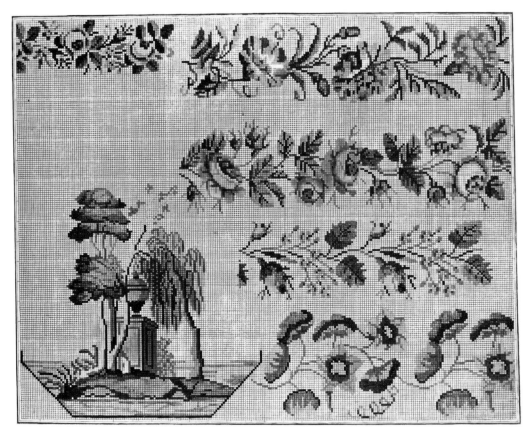

Berlin pattern, Fr. Campo, Nurnberg, with typical borders and urn on pedestal.

of point paper so that they could be used as needlepoint patterns. This, of course, made the patterns much more elaborate and detailed as the artists endeavored to include every detail they could to make the reproduction in wool or silk more true. Historical, mythological and biblical paintings were the favorite ones to be copied, with Landseer's paintings becoming a great favorite as the fad grew and reached England's shores. It is said that the patterns acquired their name of Berlin patterns when they reached England, for the obvious reason that many were made there.

Wittich patterns are most often of people against an elaborate outdoor background, rarely did they offer floral borders or bouquets. The patterns were painted by relatively unskilled women who reportedly used square-tipped brushes to properly fill the squares. One nineteenth century author claims that at one time twelve hundred people were employed to fill the great demand for patterns. The fad did not really catch on in England until 1820; it lasted about forty years in Europe and England and about ten years more in America.

Godey's Lady's Book in 1831 described Berlin patterns this way: "Paper patterns, covered with black cross lines, to represent the threads of canvass, and painted on the squares in the proper colours, may be bought at the worsted-shops." Patterns were sold, used and then sometimes returned to the seller to be resold. Exceptionally fine

LEFT: Berlin pattern on blue paper, published by P. Trube. RIGHT: Berlin pattern made for the American market.

patterns cost as much in England as forty pounds; however, in the 1860's when the fad was on the wane, a pattern could be had for fifty cents in America. Favorite patterns were glued to a piece of coarse cotton to protect them, others were cut up into fragments to be shared with friends.

The first Berlin patterns were engraved on white paper, later patterns, after 1840 or 1850, were sometimes produced on blue paper. They all have the embossed border of an engraving. Not all Berlin patterns came from Berlin, though obviously that was the center of pattern manufacture. Vienna had a publisher by the name of H. F. Muller and Nurnberg had Fr. Campe and A. P. Eisen. Besides Philipson and Wittich, Berlin publishers were P. Trube and A. Grunthal. Some patterns were also published in Paris. Augustin Legrand printed the date on the patterns he published, an unusual thing to do in that business. French patterns are usually of separate little objects, several to a page. Dogs seemed to be a favored subject.

In Holland some exquisite floral patterns were published, unfortunately the publisher was rarely marked nor was the city of origin. One can only determine the origin by the water mark on the paper.

Berlin pattern by Vallardi, Paris.

Dutch ladies enjoyed a yearbook very similar to the German one aforementioned. The Dutch yearbook was actually semi-annual, perhaps eight in all were published over a period covering 1821 to 1826. Besides the usual interesting things to make, the *Penelope of Maandwerk* by A. B. Van Meerten also devoted a considerable number of pages to moral and religious essays.

It is quite difficult to date a Berlin pattern. Philipson's 1803 patterns were just as "busy" as the repeat or diaper patterns of the 1860's. Unless the pattern says something like "Union Forever" or is a likeness of the Prince of Wales as a baby there is no rule-of-thumb way to determine the date. Later patterns given out as premiums from such magazines as *Peterson's* in the United States or the *Young Ladies' Journal* in England have the date of the issue they came in printed on them and are obviously printed, not engraved or hand colored.

The first Berlin patterns were used for needlework done with silk on fine silk canvas or on cloth with canvas basted over it as a stitch guide. They were also used for bead patterns as well as knitting patterns. After the German Zephyr wool was developed, the patterns were more or less exclusively used with wool, with certain details such as faces and arms or clothing occasionally worked in silk. The stitches used at first were the tent stitch and the Gobelin. The German Zephyr wool, being coarser than crewel wool, required a heavier canvas. Though the authorities differ on the date it is safe to say that between 1820 and 1830 many new and larger mesh canvases came on the market, capable of supporting the heavier wool. Hargreaves' and Arkwright's spinning inventions of the 1760's and Crompton's spinning mule in 1779 made it possible to spin a stronger and more evenly spun thread which in turn made it possible to weave a firmer and more even count canvas, thus permitting the use of a heavier wool than crewel, i.e. worsted Berlin wool.

The fine silk canvas used at the beginning of the Berlin craze was known as Berlin canvas. Miss Lambert in her needlework book of

1842 said that "the threads of silk canvas are formed by a fine silk wound round a cotton fibre." In her day silk canvas could be had from twenty-one mesh to the inch to forty mesh, the colors available were white, claret, black and primrose. The use of such a fine silk canvas meant that filling in the grounds or background was not necessary, a piece of silk fabric laid behind the work was considered sufficient. Perhaps because silk was so expensive it did not continue in general use. A fine woolen canvas from Germany was also used at the same time, available in the same colors as the silk canvas.

By the 1830's, the canvas made by the French was considered the best though the patterns and the wool from Germany were still

Needlepoint bag made by a member of the Ogden family, c. 1840, probably from little Berlin pattern motifs.

ABOVE: Detail of an eagle on a sampler wrought by Phebe Ann Hewlitt. The sampler is a genealogical record of the Henry Aves family, 1805–1837. Draw thread technique, silk on satin.

BELOW: Needlepoint bag made by a member of the Ogden family. Note that the background is unworked. The eagle is obviously the same one as the Hewlitt sampler eagle (above), worked in slightly different colors.

The star of Bethlehem

Brighter than the rising day
When the sun of glory shines,
Brighter than the diamond's ray
Sparkling in Golconda's mines
Beaming through the clouds of woe
Smiles in Mercy's diadem
On the guilty world below
The Star that rose in Bethlehem

Elizabeth Orme

Nov 9th
1833
Age 9

LEFT: Sampler of Elizabeth Orme, 1833. Cross stitch, brightly colored silk on linen.

BELOW: Sampler of Mary Louise McCully, 1840. Cross stitch, Berlin wool on cotton canvas.

Mary Louise McCully, wrought this in the ninth year of her age.

Patterson. 1840

considered the finest in their fields. England and Germany made a cotton canvas too, but the German canvas was considered inferior because it was not very strong. The German canvas had every tenth thread in yellow to facilitate the counting out of the Berlin patterns. Later in the century that yellow thread would change to blue, and the single thread of the canvas would multiply to two, and by 1877 a two-thread German cotton canvas would be known as Berlin canvas. It is well to mention here that the using of the name Berlin canvas for two different kinds of canvas at two different times is typical of the confusions in needlework history.

One-thread canvas was called common canvas and later on undivided canvas. Two-thread canvas was called just that or penelope canvas or, as mentioned above, Berlin canvas. A charming story about

Both sides of a handbag, American, early 19th century. Cross stitch, worked in polychrome wools, white thread and gilt beads.

penelope canvas has been circulating since Mrs. Owen collaborated with the Countess of Wilton on their book, *The Illuminated Book of Needlework* (1847). Mrs. Owen says that Penelope, the wife of Ulysses, was "beset by suitors" while he was away. She told them that when she finished "her piece of tapestry" she would choose one of the suitors. Each night she would undo her day's work, thereby stalling for more time. Mrs. Owen felt that this story might account for the canvas being called penelope because it looks as if work has just been picked out of it. The only flaw in this theory is that Penelope, according to *The Odyssey*, was weaving, not embroidering.

Of penelope canvas or two-thread canvas Miss Lambert says: "For very fine cross stitch, it is certainly unobjectionable and more easily seen; but generally speaking, the work produced upon it has not the even pearly appearance of that done over the usual canvas." Before penelope was popular it was the custom just to work over two threads instead of one if one's wool was heavier than one's canvas, and cross stitch was nearly always done this way.

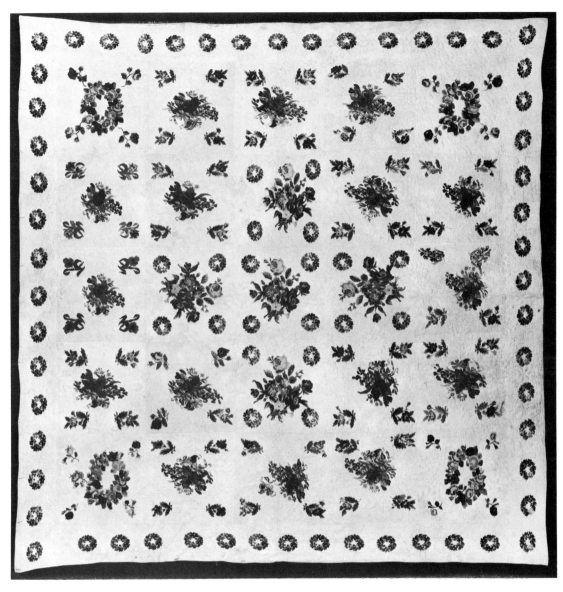

Coverlet, quilted and embroidered; the white cotton ground is quilted in a pattern of grapes and flowers on which bouquets, wreaths and garlands, primarily in shades of mauve and purple with sage-green foliage, have been done in Berlin work. The flowers were worked over canvas, the threads of which were pulled out when the work was completed.

LEFT: Piano stool from the John Marshall House, Richmond, Virginia. The wool has worn away from the needlepoint seat, exposing the lines of the design drawn on the canvas. The needlework was done by a member of the Marshall family, c. 1800.

Mosaic canvas was considered the finest canvas available of any fiber in number of mesh per inch, it was made of silk, cotton, hemp and wool. In France, a flattened canvas was produced by running it through heavy rollers. It was thought that this made it easier to mark the pattern on it. Miss Lambert felt that the flattening of the thread did not improve the appearance of the finished work. She mentions a needlework house in Paris which, after the design had been drawn on the flattened canvas, then outlined each object in the design with cotton thread of the appropriate color. Another novelty canvas was produced in England in which the threads of the

Seat of stool, upholstered with embroidered horsehair, c. 1830–1840.

warp and weft were unequal in size. It was intended to be used for the Gobelin stitch (which is worked vertically over two threads). Because Berlin patterns were made for a square meshed canvas, and this was a rectangular mesh, the resulting work was thus distorted and this canvas did not last long on the market.

One novelty which lasted into the twentieth century was not really a canvas, but paper. Bristol board or perforated cardboard first appeared about 1820 and was still being sold in 1905. It was made of a good grade of cardboard with holes punched in it in regular rows, and it was meant to be used in the same way as canvas. Its advantages were that it required no grounding, and that it "cost but a trifle." It was available in many sizes, from twenty-eight holes to the inch to ten holes to the inch, and in many colors including embossed tinsel and gold, though white was preferred. The stitches used were the tent stitch and the cross stitch, but as the century progressed, satin stitch was used more and more. At first it was used mainly for bookmarks and pictures, but with the Victorian mania for making trivia it was soon put to use for stamp houses, letter holders, dust cloth holders, waste baskets, card baskets, all sorts of needle cases, cigar cases and work boxes. Bristol board was worked in cotton thread and wool generally, but occasionally in silk and chenille and even in beads. Religious mottoes were great favorites for bookmarks such as: "It is I, Be not Afraid;" "Hope on, Hope Ever;" and "The Lord is in His Holy Temple." The all-time favorite was a bible bookmark, marked simply "Holy Bible." Rebus mottoes were done with "Come to" and then a church was pictured beneath. Sentiment received its due with "Forget Me Not" and "Love." Doing mottoes evidently delighted so many needlewomen that the Parker Company patented a line of large (9 x 21 inches) mottoes with the motto printed in black with a few flowers and leaves as trim. The mottoes were ordered by number, #121 being "We Mourn Our Loss" with an oval in the center in which to paste a picture of the dear departed. The craze for this kind of work came late in the century. The mottoes were framed in a rustic frame and sometimes were backed with tinsel or colored paper.

Starting about 1850, confusion began to reign in the canvas world. Both the French and the English began to give catalogue numbers to the different mesh canvases, which sounds harmless enough. The only trouble was that the English numbers differed from the French, and none of them corresponded to the number of mesh per inch. For example, in English canvas a number 16 had nine mesh to the inch, but a French canvas of the same number (16) had nineteen mesh to the inch. A trip to one's Berlin shop must have been a confusing experience. (See appendix for canvas numbers and mesh.)

Berlin patterns changed the wool industry as well as the canvas industry. English worsted had formerly filled the wool needs for the continental embroideress, but with the expansion of trade after the Congress of Vienna and the unification of the Germanic states, the wool men of Saxony took over the market with their German Zephyr manufactured in Gotha of merino sheep wool. German Zephyr was a softer and finer wool than the English and was capable of taking a better dye, therefore the color range was increased. With a wider range of colors demanded by the Berlin Muster Maler, the German wool answered an immediate need. It is said that there were over one thousand shades. Whenever Berlin wool is referred to the German merino zephyr is meant.

The English continued to supply wool for the embroideress but it was never as well thought of as the German; their lambswool and worsted were used for coarser work and for background fillings, their worsted was used most often for rugs. The Germans also made a worsted which they called Hamburgh wool and again their dyes were excellent. It was used when a coarse wool was needed. The German Hamburgh wool was imitated by the English and was called Hamburgh worsted, and was considered inferior to the real thing.

ABOVE: Waistcoat worn by Commodore Alfred E. Grey of the Pacific Mail Steamship Company, a native of Richmond, Virginia, and later a resident of Brooklyn, New York. American, c. 1835–1840. It is worked in tent stitch, in a skillfully matched geometric pattern.

RIGHT: Bristol board bookmark.

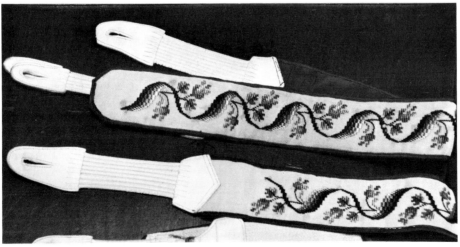

Suspenders with needlepoint worked in silk, the background not filled in.

Tremendous amounts of German wools were imported into the United States as early as the 1820's. In 1854 Mrs. Ann Stephens, a well-known writer of the time on needlework subjects, wrote in *Frank Leslie's Portfolio of Fancy Needlework* that quite a bit of "Berlin" wool was manufactured in the United States and that its quality was good. Mrs. Stephens goes on to say that Berlin wool came in only two sizes, four thread and eight thread, "unless the latter is specified in receipts (sic) the other is always implied." It was also known as single and double Berlin, and confusingly also called double zephyr. In 1877, Mrs. Annie Frost wrote in her book, *The Ladies' Guide to Needle Work*, that Berlin wool came in three degrees of fineness, single, double and split zephyr.

Another wool occasionally employed for embroidery was called Fleecy. Both the Germans and the English produced it and both had their partisans as to respective quality. Fleecy was really meant for knitting and crochet, but it became very popular for use in raised work when that came into style, about which more later. It was made in two weights, superfine and common, which came in multiple threads from two to twelve. It was less expensive than real Berlin wool.

Shaded wool or variegated wool appeared in the late 1850's. It is still being sold today in worsted for knitting purposes. It is shaded from dark to light in one color, this result being obtained by dipping the wool bit by bit deeper and deeper into the dye vat.

Another wool came on the scene around 1870, called castor wool. References to it include mention of petit point and also coarse canvas, but it is difficult to infer just what weight wool it was or whether castor might not be just a trade name.

Crewel wool made its comeback about 1875 with the return of interest in crewel-style stitching which preceded the beginnings of Art Needlework.

Fluted embroidery or Orné, known from about 1850 to 1870, ap-

Chair seat of English origin which illustrates the colors and patterns favored c. 1860. The background is worked in the Smyrna cross stitch for which there was a fad in the United States in 1862.

Phillips pattern with flowers and conventionalized border.

Bargello purse, 18th century.

pears to have been a patent type of needlepoint whereby a special canvas was matched with specially dyed wools. The canvas was worked from the center out to the edges right and left, the wools being so dyed that they formed a picture or design as they were worked over the canvas. The same type of wool was available for knitting and crochet, though the results were reported to be not as good. The wool itself was known as an Orné ball.

Before 1856 all dyes were of plant origin, it was then that William Henry Perkin (later Sir William) invented the first artificial dye stuff developed for commercial use while working with a coal tar derivitive, aniline. He named the dye stuff mauve or mauveine, which dyed silk a reddish-violet and on cotton produced a bluer shade. The color captured the interest of the fashion world and a "mauve period" was launched. Magenta was developed in France in 1859, rosaniline blue, methyl violet, Hoffman's violet, aniline black and aldehyde green followed in the next decade. By 1869 Thomas Love of Philadelphia was instructing American dyers in the art of aniline dyeing in a book called *The Art of Dyeing, Cleaning and Scouring and Finishing,* and he included yellow and orange in his list of aniline dyes. The significance of this information is that most of the poor taste in colors in Berlin wool work has been attributed to the introduction of aniline dyes. Consider-

Pincushion in the form of a bird, only two inches high. Made of silk by a member of the Ogden family.

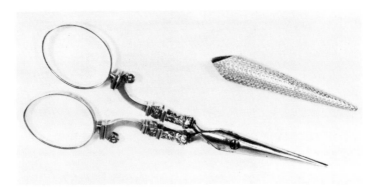

Scissors, steel blades with gold handles and finger rings; gold honeycomb embossed cover fits over the blades, 19th century.

ing the dates of aniline dye development it is not fair to blame anything pre-1860 on anilines, it was just plain bad taste.

Various kinds of silk were used for Berlin work, each having its own period of popularity. Dacca silk, a twisted silk, was used at first on the fine Berlin canvas. Mitorse was a half-twisted silk used at the same time. Floss silk enjoyed the longest popularity, it came in several weights, was untwisted and was made from the best silk. Filoselle silk was made from the poorer quality silk and was not considered pure silk. Filoselle was used, according to Mrs. Pullan, author of *The Lady's Manual of Fancy Work* (1857), "in the coarser kinds of Berlin-work" and was "nearly equal in thickness to 8 thread Berlin wool."

In reference to silk, one sometimes sees the words *ombre* and *chine* in books of the past century. Chine means that the shading in silk was done in two or more colors, ombre means that the shading was done in one color.

One of the problems that needleworkers of the nineteenth century faced was the running of the color in wools and silks. It was recommended that one should wear an apron over one's lap when one worked, to protect one's clothes as well as the embroidery materials. The use of bran and hot water on one's hands, then drying them carefully, was one remedy if sweat on the hands made the silks and wools run. Another problem was the cost of materials, silk was more expensive than wool. To economize, one could work one stroke of the cross stitch in wool, and the top stroke in silk.

Chenille was used mainly as an accent material in the nineteenth century, though it was sometimes the only material used for a Bristol board picture. In Berlin pictures one finds it as the fur on a nobleman's collar or the short hair of a baby's head or a fluffy kitten's tail; the effect was not as dreadful as one would expect. Its greatest popularity was in the second half of the century, after its price decreased. Before 1850 it was considered one of the most expensive materials in embroidery according to Miss Lambert, but by 1880 woolen chenille was advertised in the *Harper's Bazar* magazine for ten cents a skein. Even if a skein was only a quarter of an ounce, that is still a modest price.

At first chenille was made only of silk but as the century progressed more and more of it was produced in wool, until by 1899 the silk was thought to be inferior to the wool. By then it had changed its name

Silver scissors hook (worn on the belt) with sheathed silver scissors and pincushion worked in queen stitch and banded in silver, Chester County, Pennsylvania, late 18th century.

Blue wool pillow worked in gold and blue silk with steel beads and colored bead trim. Blue silk back, white and gray grapes in bead work in the center, 1850.

to Arrasene. For canvas work a fairly fine weight was used in a wide-eyed needle, in short lengths. Care was required in working it so that the fuzz did not wear off and so that it did not become crushed. Arrasene could also be purchased with wire in it.

The fancy for bead work started in the eighteenth century but its greatest popularity was coincidental with the rise of interest in Berlin patterns in the nineteenth century. Bead work was done at first on fairly fine canvas, as was Berlin work, but as the fad for it caught on, the canvas used became coarser. The beads were attached to the canvas with a half cross stitch, using a tightly twisted cotton thread, sometimes waxed, or a silk thread. The beads were sold by the bunch and sometimes by the tiny pot, they were made of glass and metal; the German beads were thought by the Americans to be the best. Jet beads became popular in the 1870's.

In England, round beads were called pound beads, presumably because they were wholesaled by the pound. Rectangular beads, rather like today's bugle beads, were called O.P. beads. It is said that there were special patterns made for O.P. bead work, the pattern squares being laid as are bricks. Steel and crystal beads were very popular, often being used together for the glittering effect they produced. By 1850 beads were used in conjunction with Berlin wool, silk and chenille for such realistic details as chain mail or sparkling water. Cushions were worked with the pattern in beads and the grounding in Berlin wool. By the 1880's the Berlin wool had been dispensed with and ink pots, paper stands, bird cages, ash "receptacles" and hat racks all had their strip of bead work trim. If the article was made of cloth, such as a pincushion, a looped bead fringe decorated the edge, either in white or crystal beads.

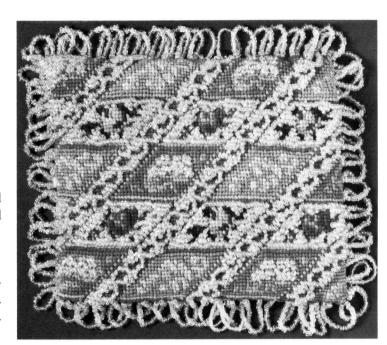

RIGHT: Bead and Berlin wool pincushion with beaded fringe, late 19th century.

BELOW: Beaded belt, probably worked from little Berlin pattern motifs, American, mid-19th century.

Berlin patterns, of course, were not the only source of design even at the height of the fad, other designs were being used with various ways of applying them to the fabric. Customarily, the design was drawn on the canvas with pen or pencil, sometimes free hand, sometimes with the drawing underneath if the fabric were thin enough and then traced. The previously mentioned pouncing method was employed too, whereby the design was pricked through the paper, then a starch- or charcoal-filled pounce was tapped over the holes. The resulting dots were connected with a "drawing liquid." Miss Lambert's recipe consisted of "flake-white, mixed with gum water, a drop of ox gall added to the color will make it work more freely." Another method of design transfer was to lay the design underneath the canvas, tack it in place, and then work right through canvas and pattern. The remains of the pattern were then torn away when the work was completed.

At the Great Exhibition of 1851 in England, the first stamped can-

LEFT: Vermeil sewing case, French. RIGHT: Gilt sewing case, American. The tools consist of punch, bodkin, needlecase, scissors and thimble.

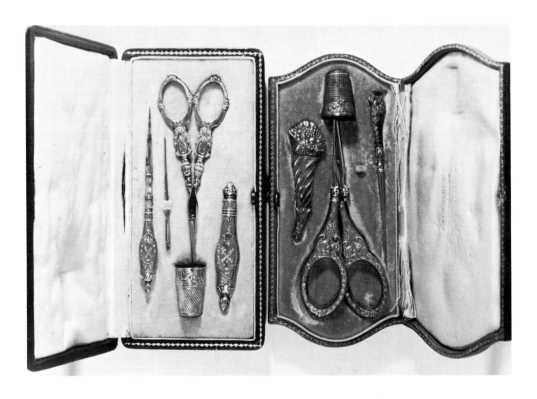

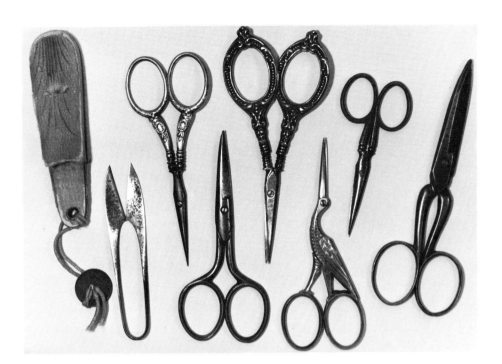

TOP: 19th century scissors; the tong-type on the left are Chinese.

CENTER: Tortoise shell sewing box. The lid shows St. Paul's Cathedral, London, painted on glass. The box is fitted with an ivory card on which to write notes, a kid silk case, two kinds of thimble, regular and hemstitching, and other tools.

RIGHT: An etui equipped with a hidden space under the thimble for wax, an ivory sliver for notes, crochet hooks and a handle to hold them, a cutwork knife, scissors, scent bottle, mirror and leather needlebook, probably English, c. 1850's.

vases were shown. By stamped it is presumed stenciled is meant, a method still very much in use today.

Mrs. Jane Weaver, a heavy contributor to *Peterson's Magazine,* gave directions for the making of transfer paper for patterns in the February 1861 issue. She suggested that one take a sheet of writing paper and rub it over with sweet oil, using a flannel cloth and being careful to wipe off any excess. Then a little color was rubbed in, unfortunately she did not specify what kind of color. The oiled sheet was to be laid on the fabric with the design to be traced over it, then an ivory knitting needle was to be employed as the stylus to trace the design. A similar technique was described in a *Harper's Bazar* of 1877 whereby a sheet of carbon paper was used instead of the oiled paper, excess carbon having first been rubbed off with a piece of bread. This method is still used today. If one did not want to ruin the original design one could use a piece of oiled tracing paper first. With all this carbon, oil and color,

19th century strawberry emeries, beeswax, tapes.

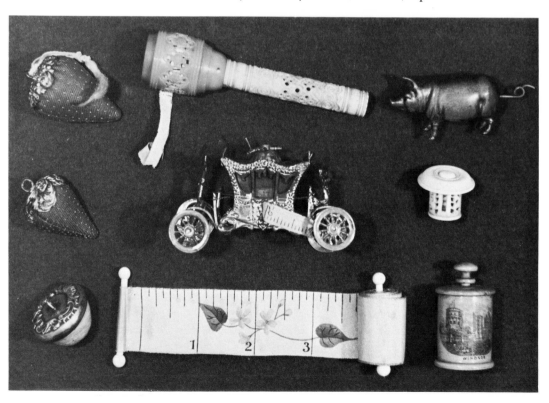

RIGHT: 19th century thimbles, ivory thread barrels and an ivory thread winder.

CENTER: 19th century thimbles. LEFT TO RIGHT: brass thimble, gold thimble with turquoise studding the border, gold thimble with initials and the date 1852, silver thimble typical of the late 19th century, all American; silver hemstitching thimble, English.

BELOW: 19th century needle cases.

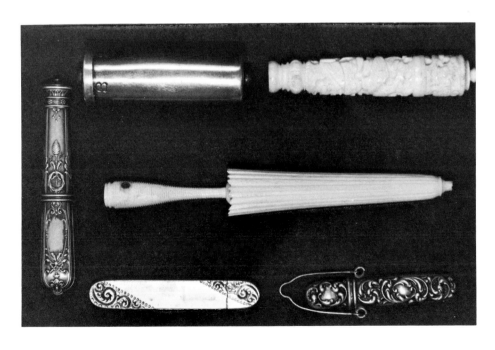

Sleeve bands, wool and beads, 19th century.

A sampler, wool and silk on cotton, mid-19th century. It was acquired in the United States but may be of European origin.

a good method of cleaning needlework was valuable. *The Dictionary of Needlework* by Caulfield and Saward, a not always reliable source of information, gave just such a recipe. After the needlework was stretched in a frame it was to be washed with a quart of water to which a tablespoon of ox-gall had been added. If one was fresh out of ox-gall, but did have some gin, that was an acceptable substitute added to a little soft soap, a quarter of a pound of soap to a half pint of gin. The needlework was then to be ironed on the wrong side while still damp.

Many needlepoint patterns were printed in black and white in the ladies' magazines after 1850. *Godey's Lady's Book* printed them in color as supplements as did *Peterson's Magazine*. *Harper's Bazar* printed patterns which showed a different symbol for each color use, not as confusing as it sounds because they stuck to floral and geometric designs rather than pictorials with many colors. *Frank Leslie's Portfolio of Fancy Needlework* also contained needlepoint patterns.

One of the small mysteries of nineteenth century needlework is what happened to all the embroidery frames that supposedly were in use. All teachers of needlework, all writers on the subject both in books and periodicals recommended the use of a frame for Berlin work as well as some other forms of embroidery. Perhaps in the reaction to the dreadful examples of needlepoint that proliferated after 1860 and also to Art Needlework, the frames were destroyed as if it were all their fault. The frames themselves were not all that awful looking in themselves, being pretty much in the style of the previous century, or very plain and functional-looking.

One method of dressing a frame that appeared often in canvas work instructions was to slant the material in the opposite direction of the slant of the stitches. The point of this was to counteract the slant or warp produced by the tent stitch. If this did not produce a straight piece of work one should paint the back of the work with isinglass water. Another technique of finishing recommended in the *Dictionary*

BIRD, IN BERLIN WORK.

Pattern from *Peterson's Magazine* and the embroidery worked from it.

of Needlework was to rub embroidery paste into the back of the work after it was blocked and pressed. The recipe for embroidery paste calls for:

> 1 oz. gum
> 1 oz. sugar candy
> small piece of alum

Cover these with cold water for four hours then mix in one ounce of flour which has been blended with water, the amount not being specified in the recipe. Pour the whole mixture into a double boiler and simmer until thick. Remove from the fire and stir until cold.

Fill-in-the-background canvases, that is, with the "executive part" already done, are not an invention of the twentieth century. Though such canvases were available earlier on the European market, this item from the 25 November 1871 *Harper's Bazar* is perhaps the first mention of their being sold directly in the United States. "Fine embroideries in wool and silk are now imported with the design done in quarter stitch, that is, four small stitches in place of one cross stitch. The purchaser then fills out the background with double cross stitch, oblong stitch, or some other simple stitch that is easily and quickly done, and is heavy enough to throw the fine work of the design into relief . . ."

The 1870's marked the end of the Berlin era and the beginning of Art Needlework. Much of the vocabulary stayed the same but new names were introduced for old varieties of embroidery. Canvas work or needlepoint was known as tapestry starting at the beginning of that decade, and cross stitch was dignified with the name of cross stitch embroidery. This was also the decade of combinations, crewel stitches were applied to canvas work as was drawn work, which was extremely well liked in its own right at that time. Some of the things made in "tapestry" and in the combinations of embroidery were carpet bags, shawl straps, lambrequins for mantels, waste baskets and window seats; and strips to use on a folding type of chair then popular. Some of the smaller items made seem pretty ridiculous to us today, for instance; dust cloth wall pockets, embroidered thermometer stands, needlepoint watch pockets to hang on the wall and, believe it or not, embroidered fly-traps!

Light colors had been used for backgrounds in the early part of the century if the background was worked at all. As the century matured the colors darkened to claret, dark green and black to support the more frantic colors of the subject matter, such as gaudy parrots, enormous roses blossoming from gothic arches and busy geometric patterns. Late in the century deep rich colors were used, making full use of the aniline dyes. On some canvas work of this period it seems that the background color has more impact than the subject.

The last quarter of the century found Persian and Egyptian motifs much admired for household items. The sunflower motif in canvas work was voguish as well as catkins done in satin stitch with the background in petit point. Strips of canvas were alternated with strips of velvet for cushions and chair seats. Light screens and banners worked in beads and canvas work decorated the parlor. The sofa might have a cushion nestling in one corner such as the one described in an 1879 issue of *Harper's Bazar*. It had alternate squares of satin applied to the canvas in a checkerboard pattern, each satin square had a flower embroidered on it. The canvas squares had another checkerboard pattern consisting of smyrna cross stitch alternating with little pom-poms, each tied on individually. Each corner of the cushion was trimmed with larger pom-poms and the sides were corded with pom-poms. The colors suggested for making this treasure were dark red, light blue and olive.

Crewel work lessons and kits began to be advertised in 1877 but it was not crewel as we know it today. The materials used were the

Picture showing Boaz with Naomi and Ruth, worked on Bristol board in Berlin wool.

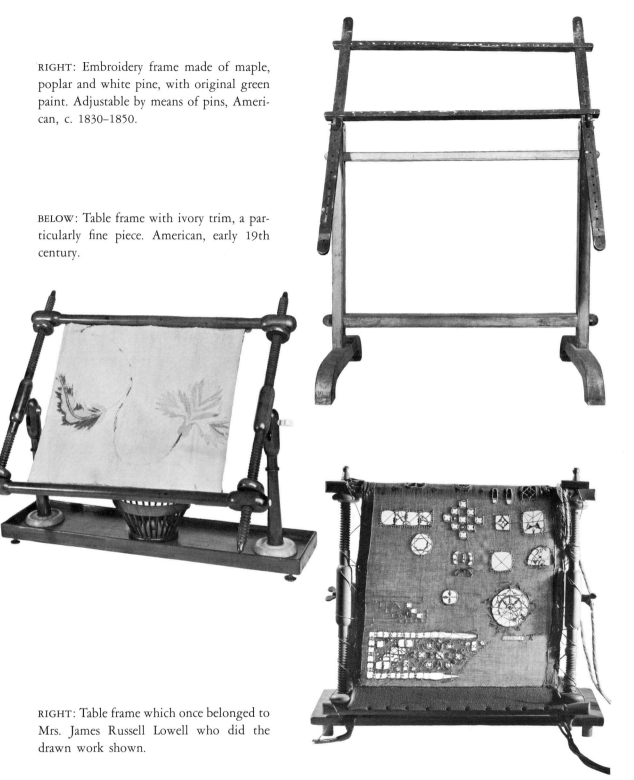

RIGHT: Embroidery frame made of maple, poplar and white pine, with original green paint. Adjustable by means of pins, American, c. 1830–1850.

BELOW: Table frame with ivory trim, a particularly fine piece. American, early 19th century.

RIGHT: Table frame which once belonged to Mrs. James Russell Lowell who did the drawn work shown.

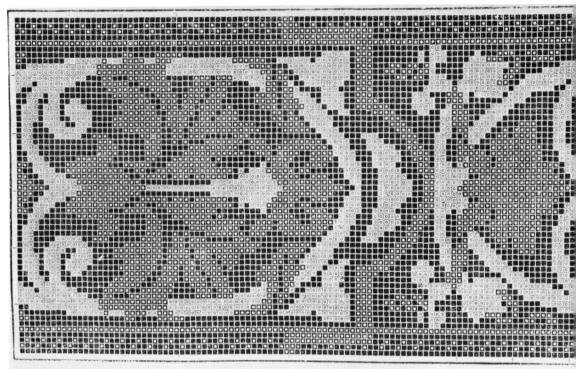

Fig. 3.—TAPESTRY DESIGN FOR COVER OF WASTE BASKET, FIG. 1.
Description of Symbols: ■ Reddish-brown Worsted; ◻ Yellow Filling Silk; ◙ Light Yellow Saddler's Silk.

Harper's Bazar pattern showing symbols for colors.

materials of Art Needlework; workhouse sheeting, hop-sacking, and crash. Linen twill was used also and according to an article in the *Harper's Bazar* of 10 February 1877, woolen materials such as serge and cloth of gold. By 1880 this type of work was commonly called Art Needlework in advertisements and the appelation of crewel had been dropped entirely. The name was borrowed from the Royal School of Art Needlework founded in England in 1872. The location of the Royal School in Kensington gave the United States the name of its favorite Art Needlework stitch, the Kensington stitch. Some of the Art Needlework was beautiful and some was worse than Berlin work at its worst. William Morris, the famous English designer, was associated with the movement there, and Candace Wheeler of the Decorative Art Society was one of the leaders in this country.

Most of the designs were floral, with the same design elements being used in various combinations in the space given. The rage for Art Needlework swept canvas work from the minds of American women. Many articles and books were written on the subject of how to design for Kensington embroidery, starter kits could be had for as little as a dollar, as shown by this advertisement in the *Harper's Bazar* of 30 January 1886: "Kensington Outfit, worth $8.80 for only $1.00 includes white powder, blue powder, poncets, needles, patterns, manual and a red satin stamped banner."

Canvas work was still done after 1880, but it was no longer *the* fashion. Mrs. Jane Weaver writing in *Peterson's Magazine* in 1882

Lambrequin with chenille tassels, last quarter 19th century.

Lacquer sewing table, made in the Orient, complete with ivory tools; first half 19th century. It was given to a friend by Stephen Decatur and returned by the heirs for display in the Decatur House.

comments that the fad for Berlin wool work is over though she thinks that there will always be a place for woolwork. Her use of the word woolwork is apt, because the best description of some of the work done at that time is woolwork. Even angora wool was put to use.

ABOVE, LEFT: Slipper holder to hang on the wall. The pocket is made of needlepoint. Exhibited at the Philadelphia Centennial Exhibition, 1876.

RIGHT: Fire or heat screen, with unworked background. The boy is lowering a kitten out of the playhouse, mid-19th century.

BELOW: Pair of footstools, mahogany frames with needlepoint and beaded upholstery.

LEFT: Chair, rosewood with needlepoint upholstery, peach-orange background, c. 1850. From the house of Ernest Fielder and his wife, née Helen Mary Hart.

RIGHT: Side chair, rosewood and mahogany in the "Elizabethan" style, c. 1850. Needlepoint seat worked by Mrs. Richard Van Wyck, née Catherine Bergen Johnson, married 1851.

It was a rare pattern that called for just tent stitch or cross stitch alone without some kind of couching, needleweaving, or threads drawn out.

The interchange of stitch names continued. A great fad for the Smyrna cross stitch flourished around 1862. Then in 1884 Smyrna work became the rage, but it was not the cross stitch that was meant, it was the canvas, Smyrna canvas, a large meshed double thread canvas. The stitch done on this canvas was a tassel loop made with a crochet hook. The *Harper's Bazar* called the plain old cross stitch in 1875 the single cross stitch. The next year fashion had changed its name in the same magazine to the Vienna cross stitch. Crewel stitches were

RIGHT: Straw work thread holder, of English origin.

BELOW: Sewing box, painted wood, decorated on the top with "Union Forever" and on the front with "Ladns (sic) Companion;" Civil War period.

adapted to canvas work but always with a new name. Thus the feather stitch appears in the 26 April 1884 *Harper's Bazar* as the coral stitch worked over tramé. The Roumanian stitch appears in 1893 as the janina stitch. Florentine embroidery or Bargello was called Hungary stitch in 1886, Pointe de Hongrie in 1891 and Pointe de Flamme in 1896 according to the *Harper's Bazar's* of those years.

Illustration from *Harper's Bazar,* June 1871. The caption reads "Like Mistress, Like Maid."

Four

SOME OLD STITCHES REVIVED

THE nineteenth century was a vintage one for fancy stitches, literally hundreds were invented. Sometimes they were given a name, sometimes not, and sometimes two or three names, which is very confusing to today's reader. Then sometimes the process worked in reverse and one name was used for two or three stitches. One must keep this in mind in any study of embroidery stitches, a diagram of the stitch must accompany the name in order to verify. However, this does not always help, because the diagram may have been printed backwards, as in Mrs. Owen's *The Illuminated Book of Needlework* where the tent stitch is diagramed as slanting downwards from the left. In the words of Miss Lambert in 1842 ". . . it is as easy to invent new stitches, as it is to invent new names for them."

The century started off serenely with the most used stitches being the tent stitch and the cross stitch. The tent stitch was then called the tent stitch or the single stitch or petit point. The cross stitch was known as the single cross stitch and by some as gros point. Now, of course, petit point and gros point refer to the *size* of the tent stitch, not the *kind* of stitch being done. As mentioned before, at first backgrounds were not worked in Berlin work, but as silk canvas was used less and cotton canvas more, a less monotonous and tedious method of filling in backgrounds than tent stitch or cross stitch was sought. Three more stitches were added to the accepted list. These were the Gobelin stitch, the Irish stitch and the German stitch.

The Cross Stitch  The Gobelin Stitch

The Gobelin stitch was also known as the tapestry stitch and was done up two mesh and over one, just as we do the slanting Gobelin today. This stitch was highly recommended for backgrounds of landscapes and was a great favorite of Berlin workers. Stitch directions were often rather bizarre in the embroidery books, one wonders what the results of the following directions for the Gobelin stitch might have looked like as given in an etiquette book printed in the early 1840's: "Bring the needle to the surface up two threads and insert it down over twenty-one threads, up three, down twenty-two; up

Sofa with needlepoint upholstery, 6 inches high, from a doll's house in the Chester County Historical Society. All the furniture in this four-room house, dated 1836, was made by a Philadelphia cabinetmaker and upholsterer named Voegler.

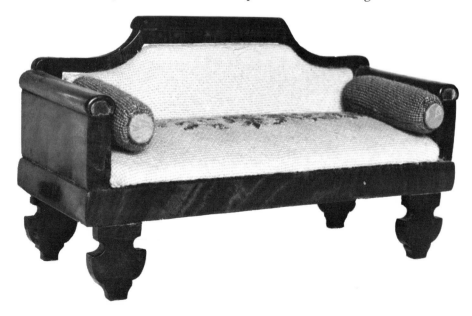

four, down twenty-three. Continue in this manner to the end of the row. The stitches may be regulated in height to accord with the subject. This stitch is adapted for large patterns."

The Irish stitch was considered strictly a grounding stitch and was recommended because of the speed with which one could work it. It is an upright stitch done over four mesh in the same manner as the brick stitch is done, and really does cover ground quickly.

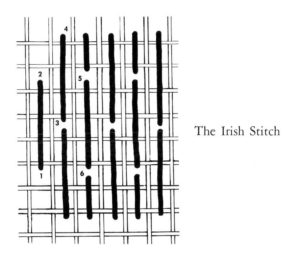

The Irish Stitch

The German stitch was another stitch suggested only for grounding. It is still a popular stitch today and is known as the diagonal mosaic stitch.

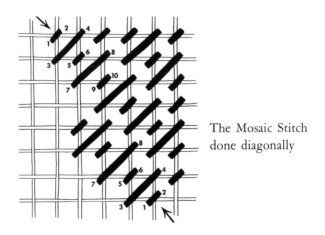

The Mosaic Stitch done diagonally

By 1845 there were many other stitches listed in the needlework books, quite a few of them were simply long single stitches taken over five or six mesh arranged in different patterns which did not cover the canvas very well. They carried such names as Windsor, Princess, Sutherland, and Willow. Others are known and used stitches of today such as the Josephine stitch, now known as the Parisian embroidery stitch, and the feather stitch now known as the fern stitch.

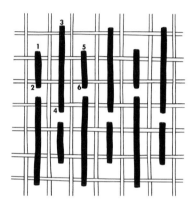

The Parisian Stitch

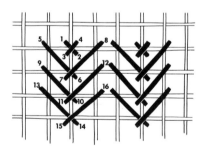

The Fern Stitch

Raised work became very much the rage in the 1840's, though it had been done before that, and its popularity continued for several decades in various forms. One might say it was turkey work all over again, the tufted stitch with a cross stitch background, but this time the tufted stitch had some shape, it was sculpted to follow the form of the subject matter. Flowers and birds, especially parrots and pigeons, were the big favorites in naturalistic colors and with lovely glass eyes (attached by means of a long wire stem through the wool) to make it more life-like.

The raised work was done over an instrument called a mesh which formed the loop of the stitch. Mesh were made of bone, boxwood and metal. Miss Lambert says that the mesh came in widths from a sixteenth of an inch to two or three inches. A groove was sometimes added to serve as a guide for the scissors when the loops were cut. The metal mesh had a sharp edge on one side so that as the mesh was withdrawn from the loops it would cut them. In appearance

Pigeons done in raised work, background in cross stitch, 1841.

it looked like an old-fashioned skate, the end of it being slightly rounded. Netting mesh could be used if a proper mesh was not available, or even a knitting needle.

Though nineteenth century needlework authors were rather notorious for borrowing from each other's work, the directions for the raised work stitch all differ. Included here are two versions, one from Mrs. Pullan's book, *The Lady's Manual of Fancy Work,* and the other from the *Dictionary of Needlework.* Mrs. Pullan's version always forms a vee on the back of the canvas, it is basically just the half cross stitch done twice in the same place. After the loop is made on this version, it should be held down to the right so that the second stitch will somewhat lock it down. Both stitches should be started from the lower left of the area to be worked, and should be worked row by row from left to right up the canvas. Both stitches should be started with the wool fastened into the backs of preceding stitches and should be finished off the same way.

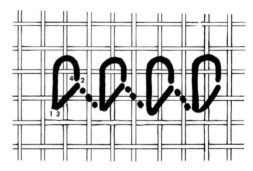

Mrs. Pullan's Raised Work Stitch

The *Dictionary* version of the raised work stitch seems to fit penelope canvas best. As with the other version it helps if one holds down the loop while the locking half cross stitch is made. The *Dictionary* calls this version the Plush stitch. It is recommended with both versions that the background stitch be worked first, then the raised work. All of the raised work stitches should be trimmed with scissors to form the plush and open the loops but this step should wait until the work is completed, otherwise uneven plush will result.

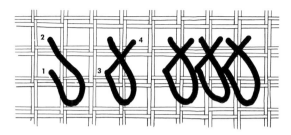

Dictionary of Needlework's Raised Work Stitch

The turkey work stitch could be used as well as either of the above two, the end result is the same, a tufted stitch.

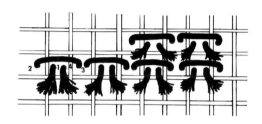

The Turkey Work Stitch

The velvet stitch became popular in the 1840's and continued in favor until the 1880's when it changed its name and emerged in *Harper's Bazar* as the closed herringbone stitch. This stitch is done over six mesh in height and is worked in several journeys over the same length of mesh, getting wider as one works. Work a row of herringbone stitch over two mesh. Cut a narrow piece of thin cardboard to cover the width of the stitches and the length of the row. Work a row of herringbone stitch over the two mesh rows over which you have laid the cardboard strip, this time covering four mesh with your stitches. Then work another row of herringbone stitch over the accumulated stack of stitches using six mesh in height. (If you will oversew an extra stitch at A and B on every stitch in the four and six mesh rows you can lock your stitches in and avoid the next step. See diagram.)

Now take some liquid latex sold as rug skid preventive (for instance RUG-STA) and paint with a fine brush the back of your rows of stitches, but do it lightly. Gum arabic or isinglass water was the material used in the old days. When it is dry, in about an hour, cut down the center of your stitches as far as the cardboard guard strip. This makes your nap. If held over a steaming tea kettle, the wool fibers fuzz up nicely, forming the velvet of the name. The stitch can be done on mono-canvas but penelope canvas is preferable.

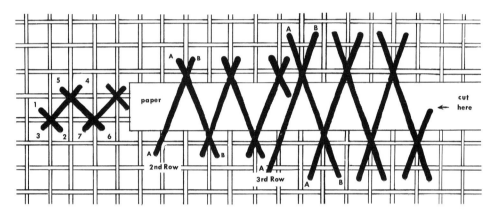

The Velvet Stitch or Closed Herringbone Stitch

The lace stitch is a misnomer, it is not so much a stitch as a pattern. The effect desired was that of lace edging, and lace border patterns were used. Netting silk in white formed the "lace" part of the pattern, black Berlin wool was used for the background. It was often used as the edging or frame to another pattern. Its popularity started in the 1840's and lasted till the '60's.

By the 1860's the stitch vocabulary of the American Berlin worker had increased considerably but old stitches were still used though perhaps not in the old way. One such stitch was the knotted stitch as it was known then. The *Harper's Bazar* of 21 March 1868 described a little light screen that could be made using this old stitch which had once been used for the fleece of the sheep in samplers. The English called it the pin stitch because it looked to them like the heads of pins, and we know it today as French knots. The new way that the knotted stitch was used was with canvas, which according to the

Bazar instructions was to be laid over a piece of linen and stretched in an embroidery frame. A knot was made in the canvas holes to form the pattern. When the work was completed the canvas was removed and the linen was framed in the light screen.

The Smyrna stitch referred to on page 105 is worked as shown below. This is not to be confused with the tassel loop made with a crochet hook on Smyrna canvas.

Two other stitches with a confusion of names are the feather stitch, later called the coral stitch worked over tramé and the Roumanian stitch, renamed the janina stitch.

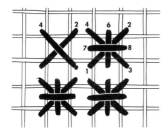

The Smyrna Stitch

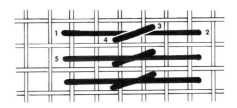

The Roumanian Stitch or Janina Stitch

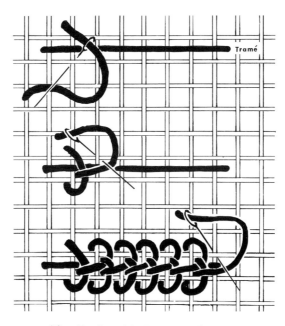

The Feather Stitch or Coral Stitch

The leviathan stitch also known as the star stitch was a much admired stitch of the late 1860's. It was used as a specimen stitch then and in the 1880's appeared again as a grounding stitch. This was achieved by omitting the outside crosses except for every other stitch.

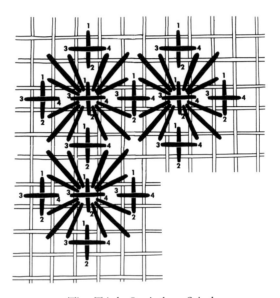

The Triple Leviathan Stitch

A similar stitch to the leviathan was shown in the *Harper's Bazar* of 27 June 1868, and as was often in the case with *Harper's* no name was given for the stitch. This one might just as well be called the flower stitch as it looks very much like one, it can only be used as a specimen. To fill in the background one must work the half cross stitch in four different directions.

Another nameless stitch which appeared in *Peterson's Magazine* in the 1860's was what we might call the reverse eyelet stitch. It must be combined with the half cross stitch in order to maintain its integrity, if done in a block as a grounding it turns into the plain old eyelet stitch. One could quarter it with a long stitch if one wished.

The "Flower" Stitch

The "Reverse Eyelet" Stitch

The fancy cross stitch is another nameless stitch from *Peterson's Magazine.* It must have the canvas match the wool just right or canvas will show through under the big cross stitch. It makes a very busy grounding.

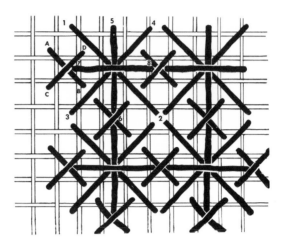

The Fancy Cross Stitch

Some of the stitches diagrammed in the ladies' magazines just won't work out on canvas no matter how much "fiddling" is done, one such being the spiral stitch which is shaped like the funnel of a tornado. Others such as the Berlin mosaic stitch look so messy when completed that they hardly seem worth the effort. This stitch consists of one square of horizontal stitches set inside a larger square of diagonally done stitches. Only those stitches that are clearly workable have been diagrammed.

Point Russe embroidery was a form of stitchery that gained some popularity in the second half of the nineteenth century. It was worked with silk and cotton thread on a counted thread fabric using long stitches to form line patterns. When the closer woven, prettier canvases such as Java canvas were used, the background was left bare. The line patterns were often combined with Berlin work or superimposed

Point Russe embroidery from a sampler done c. 1860.

in silk floss. *Harper's Bazar* showed a stitch in October of 1869 which puts one in mind of Point Russe, and is in fact called the Point Russe stitch. It can be worked as a grounding stitch or as a specimen. It is tedious to work as a grounding, but the result is quite Victorian looking.

The Point Russe Stitch

The Point Russe Stitch
Quartered with long stitches

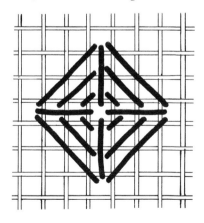

The following are six variations of the cross stitch as shown in the *Harper's Bazar* from 1871 to 1892 and also from the *Dictionary of Needlework* by Saward and Caulfield.

The woven cross stitch is essentially four long stitches interwoven covering six mesh one way and four the other. A full strand of Persian wool would be needed to cover a fourteen mesh canvas. The stitch is a specimen stitch unless it is done in rows with half cross stitches filling in the spaces.

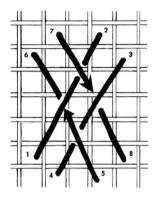

The Woven Cross Stitch

The woven cross stitch square can be worked both as a specimen or as a grounding. It is very attractive done in two colors. It is worked in diagonal rows when used as a grounding.

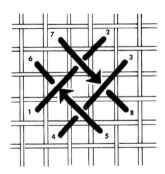

The Woven Cross Stitch Square

The tied down cross stitch can be worked in diagonal rows as a grounding or alone as a specimen. Just be sure that all the top crosses cross in the same direction for a neat finished look.

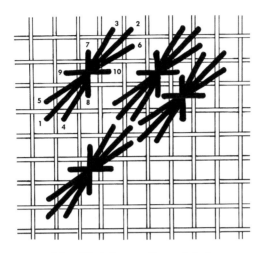

The Tied Down Cross Stitch

The slanting cross stitch uses two different strandings of wool to achieve its effect. The first trip on fourteen mesh canvas would be taken with a full strand of Persian wool. On the second journey only two threads of the three-thread strand will be needed.

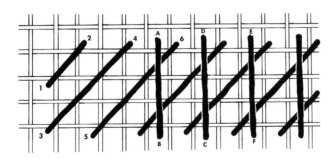

The Slanting Cross Stitch

The long cross stitch will be one that you will think you always knew once you try it. It makes a high ridged braid, and is a good rug stitch.

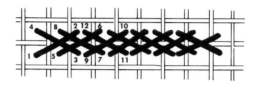

The Long Cross Stitch

The closed cat stitch is very much like the herringbone stitch and the long armed cross or Greek stitch, but there is a difference if you will compare them. It makes a tight braid and works best as a specimen row rather than a grounding. This stitch actually did appear in 1892 under the above name.

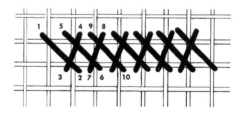

The Closed Cat Stitch

The next two stitches should be called super-cross stitches in that they cover so many mesh. They are very similar in appearance, but you will see the difference when you go to work them. The first stitch in point of time (1873) is the triple cross stitch. The background of half cross stitch must be worked first in order that the stitch itself doesn't look nibbled. Leave a space empty six mesh each way, two mesh wide. The very long stitches in the diagram are done right into the grounding of half cross stitch. The final cross stitch on top might be of another color.

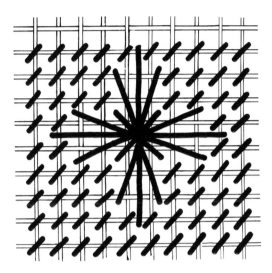

The Triple Cross Stitch

The second super-cross stitch is the check stitch which makes a very tweedy-looking grounding but can be used alone. It does not break down well into halves or quarters so that the space allotted for it must fit the stitch, rather than the stitch accommodating to the space. Be careful that you cross the stitch the same way each time. A small cross stitch may be added to tie down the big cross if so desired. (See next page.)

The next four stitches have nothing in common except that one must pay attention to every stitch when one works them, mistakes are easily made but the results are very interesting. (Pages 124–126.)

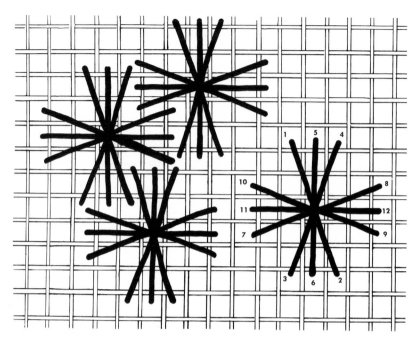

The Check Stitch

The diagonal knit stitch is a firm quick grounding stitch. It really does look like knitting. Be careful not to work it too tightly so that it warps the canvas.

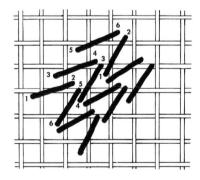

The Diagonal Knit Stitch

The laced chain stitch is a very difficult stitch to work. It can be worked with two needles threaded in different colors and from either end. To start, work two Gobelin stitches in every other mesh for one row. Then pick one of the Gobelin stitches from each side of the blank mesh to start the chain. If you can keep in mind that your needle returns to the hole it came out of for each stitch, and that you must pick up a part of each of the two stitches in the row behind, you will achieve success. You will need a heavier strand of wool than you would expect to cover the canvas.

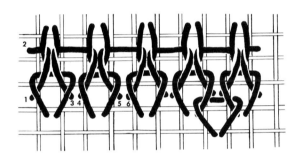

The Laced Chain Stitch

Mrs. Jane Weaver of *Peterson's Magazine* introduced Pointe de Tresse in the January of 1888 issue. The stitch produces quite a large braid. It is best to work the stitch economically, that is in one mesh and out the one next door, otherwise one has as much bulky braid on the back of the canvas as on the front. The stitches do not slip even on mono-canvas if they are not worked too tightly. The braid can consist of groups of three consecutive stitches or six consecutive stitches. The diagram shows three.

The vertical tramé stitch is a penelope canvas stitch, though it can be done on mono-canvas, because penelope is just right for tramming. The stitch has a better appearance if alternate strips of

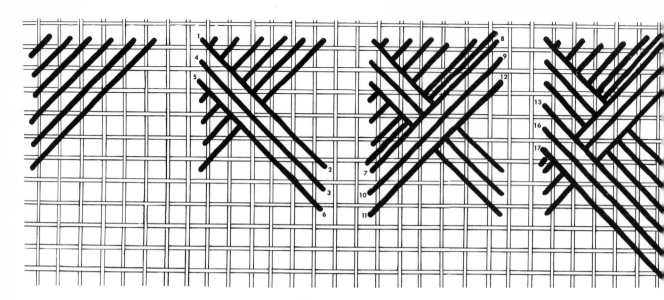

The Pointe de Tresse Stitch

half cross stitch separate the strips of vertical tramé stitch. One can do the tramé first and then return to do the tying down half cross stitches.

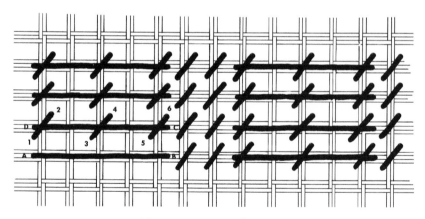

The Vertical Tramé Stitch

The manufacture of useful handwork items in the nineteenth century was not so much a necessity as it was a form of entertainment and also a very proper thing for a well-bred young lady to do with her free time. Magazine editors were constantly trying to find new and novel items for their readers to make. Some of the items were really quite frivolous but had a useful "intention". The ribbon work for which directions appeared in *Godey's Lady's Book* in May of 1849 is an example of frivolous usefulness. A piece of undivided canvas was to have every other thread cut and drawn out, thus making it larger in mesh. Then fine ribbon was to be wound or "sewn over" every thread. It was suggested that a different color ribbon should be used for the vertical and horizontal threads. When the winding was finished a wider piece of ribbon was used to bind the edges. The finished product could be used for a candle or lamp mat.

There are other more practical and attractive ways of using canvas than the ones above which were current in the nineteenth century. Some of the ways are quite adaptable to today's uses and materials. For want of a proper nineteenth century name the title of drawthread needlepoint has been tacked on a favorite technique of the very early Berlin era. Miss Lambert and Mrs. Pullan both wrote about framing cloth and canvas together and working through both, but neither author gave the practice a name. The idea of the technique is that after the pattern is completed through both fabrics, the work is unframed and the canvas threads are pulled out one by one leaving the needlepoint (or cross stitch) sitting up by itself on the cloth. Some needlewomen felt that it was better to clip off the unused canvas close to the subject. If the pattern were not solid stitching, little patches of canvas would show. This was solved by stitching over these areas with the same color wool or silk as the background cloth. Both wool cloth and satin were used as backgrounds for this type of work. Raised work was also worked this way sometimes.

Obviously this technique has a use today, if only to avoid filling in a tedious background. There would be no matching of wool to upholstery fabric if the fabric itself is used. Valances, chair seats, and cushions could be made to coordinate with rug or curtain patterns.

Though few of the early authors mention it, careful examination

Draw thread owl worked on velveteen. Some of the horizontal and vertical threads have been pulled out.

of existing work shows that a lining of thin but firm cotton has been used under the work. A piece of lawn will fit the bill today. Any reasonably firm cloth will do as the backgrounding, upholstery silk, broadcloth, velveteen, or a closely woven synthetic. Work a sample to find out what weight wool, canvas and fabric combination works the best.

Lay the lawn out first, then the fabric, and then the canvas, tack and baste them so that you will have no puckers in your layers. The old rule was that the cloth should be smaller than the canvas because of stretching, today it is the canvas that is apt to give. Using good stout carpet thread, sew your "sandwich" into the frame. Start your needlepoint from the center of the pattern and work out to the edges, or from top to bottom, but do not skip about from place to place on the canvas. There is just a little give in this sandwich and the work must proceed steadily from the worked area out.

When the needlepoint is finished, clip the canvas to within one inch and a half of the subject. Ravel the canvas all around and then firmly pull the threads out one by one. Put your hand on the work and pull straight out, not up, or you will stretch the stitches on the edge. Steam and block if necessary. Half cross stitch or cross stitch are recommended for use with this technique, a fancy stitch can be used but not on the edges if a "hard" edge is desired.

Gum arabic was the important ingredient in the next technique. In 1858, Sarah Hale gave directions in the *Godey's Lady's Book* for a dahlia pen wiper. The petals were of raised Berlin work. She wrote; "cut the canvas close to the edge, and blacken with ink the edge of the canvas and with a camel's hair brush slightly gum the edge and back of the leaf." Then the pile was cut on each petal. *Harper's Bazar* had directions in 1878 for a tidy made of maroon plush. A twined leaf design was to be worked in cross stitch on coarse canvas. The back of the work was then to be covered with gum arabic and the unworked canvas would be cut away. The work was then to be "applied" to the maroon plush and the edges trimmed with yellow silk cord.

The pen wiper may not be of much interest in the modern world of ball-point pens, but the tidy idea has some application. For gum arabic one can substitute liquid latex. Do not buy latex in a spray can, it does not work for this purpose.

The thick white fluid can be painted on the canvas and will be dry within six hours. If it is painted on after the canvas is worked, care must be taken that it does not soak into the wool through to the front; lightly does it. The reason for using latex on canvas is, of course, to keep the canvas from fraying or unweaving at the edges. After a canvas has been painted it is possible but rather difficult to pull a thread from the edge. One can cut right to the very edge

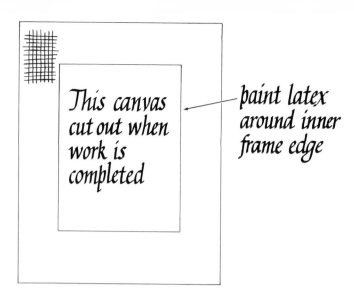

This canvas cut out when work is completed

paint latex around inner frame edge

of stitching and the canvas holds its shape, the stitches do not slip or fall off the short canvas threads.

Using this technique one could make motifs for sofa cushions or petit point emblems for blazers. Applying "slips" of needlepoint dates back to Elizabethan times, as noted earlier.

Mrs. Pullan had a suggestion for doing the reverse of this technique. She recommended that ladies with artistic talent apply white silk to the canvas for the face and other skin areas or "limbs" and that these areas should then be painted "with almost as careful a finish as a miniature." Sometimes the artistic ladies worked the face in fleshy tones without features and then painted the features right on top of the stitches.

The canvas used for making slips should be of a fairly fine mesh, unless you can find a shop that carries cross stitch canvas. This canvas, which is two-thread, looks just like the old Berlin canvas in that it has a blue thread every ten mesh. It is made of a very light cotton thread, when used for our present purposes this is an advantage because it does not add bulk under the wool. It costs but a trifle, as they were so fond of saying in the 1880's, and comes in mesh from about ten to the inch to sixteen to the inch.

Draw your design on the canvas with acrylic paints, or crayon (carefully ironed on paper towels to remove excess wax) and then paint the outside outline with latex, covering a couple of mesh inside the border and at least one outside. On one's first piece try to keep the curves to a minimum. An angle that goes up from right to left will have to have the half cross stitch reversed. That is, the stitch will follow the slant of the angle. Don't worry, the stitches will all go together all right. The extreme tips of corners must be carefully handled so that the end stitch won't fall off the canvas when the excess canvas edge is cut off.

When the stitching is finished, block first and then cut the canvas off as close to the stitching as you possibly can. Pin it to the fabric on which you intend to use it and blind stitch it on. If you have

Needlepoint slip. The design edges were painted with liquid latex before it was worked. When the design was finished, the excess canvas was carefully clipped off and the design was blind stitched to the velveteen.

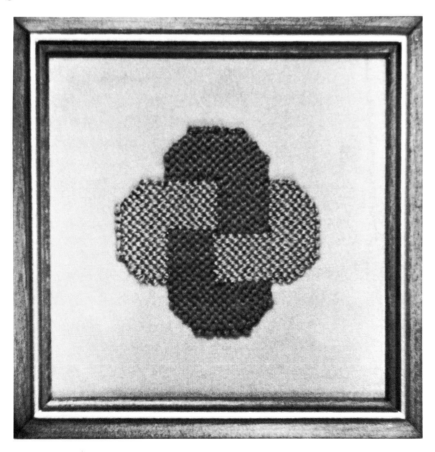

Imitation needlepoint. On the left is real needlepoint, on the right at the bottom, the imitation needlepoint is still whole. At upper right, the laid-down threads of wool have become un-machine-stitched.

cut closely enough the cut canvas stubs should not show. Couching a matching thread of wool around the edge should remedy the situation if this does occur.

Liquid latex can be used on the edges of the canvas on any project to keep the canvas from ravelling. It does not catch the wool as one works over it. It also can be used for frame edges. Paint the inside edge, work the stitches, cut out the picture area canvas and work a long cross stitch or buttonhole stitch over the edge to keep it tight. Work right over and into the first row of stitching.

Mosaic tapestry or damask embroidery has been described in a previous book of the author's under the name of Gobelin tramé.*

* *Needlepoint.* Charles Scribner's Sons, 1964.

This name was given to the technique because that is essentially what it is. A thread or braid is trammed down, and a Gobelin stitch is then worked over it in rows or in a pattern. Mrs. Ann S. Stephens, one of the editors of *Peterson's Magazine,* stated in the May 1856 issue that braid made of straw was suitable for this type of work as well as gold or silver braid. She says that the canvas mesh must be chosen "of such a size that two threads will be covered by the width of the braid."

The important thing with this stitch or technique is that the wool cover the canvas. Two threads of tapestry wool will cover one double line of mesh on ten mesh to the inch penelope. The tramé should not be done as is customary, that is at random across the canvas, because the gaps between the tramé stitches would show. It should be laid all the way across the area you want covered in one long stitch.

Harper's Bazar suggests using chenille as the tramé in the directions for the border of a footstool in their 25 September 1869 issue. It further suggests using a cross stitch instead of the upright Gobelin. The 10 September 1870 issue in directions for a sofa cushion

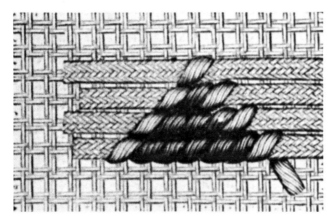

Gold braid tramé, illustration from *Harper's Bazar,* October 1869. The half-cross stitch is used instead of Gobelin.

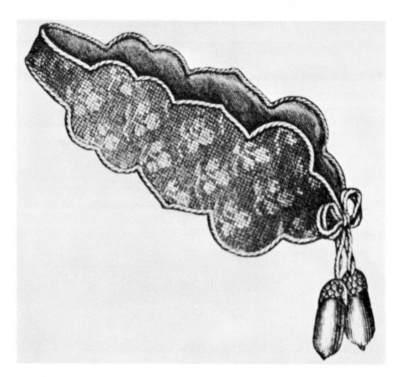

Needlepoint curtain tie-back from *Harper's Bazar,*
July 1871. This could be reproduced today using
Rug-sta for the edges, and cording.

Hat rack with needlepoint trim on the base, from
Harper's Bazar.

using gold braid as the tramé recommends that the work be done in a frame, a valid suggestion if a large area is to be covered.

The 1880's brought a great interest in drawn work and it was often combined with needlepoint for chair tidies, or chair backs which tied on to the back of a chair to protect the upholstery from some of the "new" hair pomades just coming on the market. Another favorite item to make with drawn work was a work bag, lined with a matching satin which peeked through the threads of the drawn canvas. Canvas was often tinted purple then, perhaps it was thought pretty enough to show.

The nineteenth century designs, including drawn work, were very

Gilt wood waste basket, the double lids and side panels are needlepoint, from *Harper's Bazar,* July, 1873.

symmetrical, but using abstract designs or just plain stripes, drawn work could be used today for such things as work bags again, a camp stool seat or possibly for grill cloth on stereo speakers. A finer canvas was formerly used for this type of work, but rug canvas is much easier on the eyes and much easier to work with. Use rug wool, which some shops happily sell by the strand, or a full strand of Persian wool for the drawn work, the background will have to be worked in rug wool to cover the canvas adequately.

The woven bar stitch is the most adaptable stitch for our purposes. Draw as many of the horizontal threads of canvas as you want. To do this, clip right in the middle of the area you plan to draw out. Pull the clipped threads back through the canvas to the end of your planned area of drawn work. Thread each mesh thread in a needle or if the ends are too short, use a crochet hook. Weave these threads

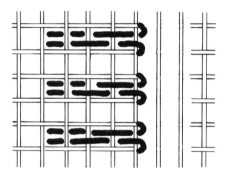

Weft canvas threads woven back into the canvas.

back at least one mesh into the background canvas. The woven-in thread should end up on the back of the canvas, clip it close.

To start working the stitch, just run a tag of wool about three inches long in and out of the canvas. It can be worked in after the work is in progress or can be stitched over when the background stitch is worked.

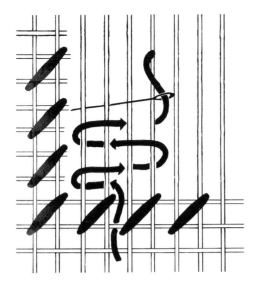

The Woven Bar Stitch

Simple patterns can be woven on canvas, using the vertical threads as the warp. The sides of the weaving can be attached to the canvas

Unmounted slippers, in black silk with white, black, silver, bronze and crystal beads. The canvas is tinted lavender, c. 1870.

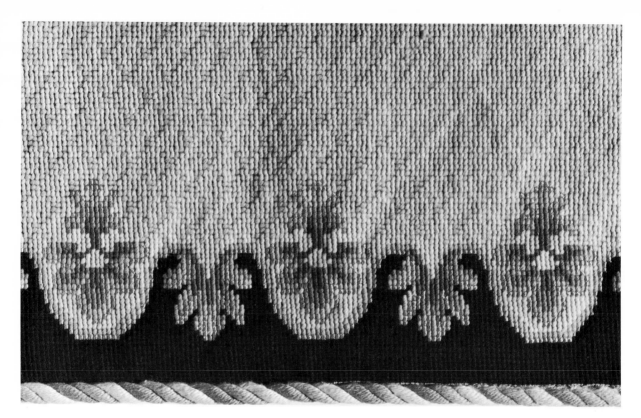

ABOVE: Detail from a needlepoint rug for a doll's house, 18 inches square. The border design is very typical of those favored in the 1860's and 1870's. It is worked in wool and silk in tent stitch; the field of the rug has a criss-cross design achieved in both color and texture by a very slight difference in the tension of the thread when the diagonal stitches were worked.

BELOW: Berlin work glasses case done in cross stitch, probably mid-19th century. Glasses had long narrow lenses then.

by working a stitch through both weaving and background and then covering it with a half cross stitch. *The Dictionary of Needlework* suggested doing tapestry by this method, but it is doubtful that much success would be achieved, there is just too much give in the canvas threads.

Detail from a prie-dieu cushion worked in wool and silk. From a convent near Frederick, Maryland, worked there c. 1870. The colors are bright, with rust and purple predominating.

Five

EPILOGUE:
FROM 1900 ON

NEEDLEPOINT did not become "a lost art" after the surge of popularity for Art Needlework, it just became a submerged art. Addie E. Heron in her book *Ladies' Work for Pleasure and Profit* (1905) shows to just what straits it was reduced:

"Berlin Embroidery was, anciently, as much in vogue as is the flat or art embroidery of the present day. In its original form, that is, wrought on canvas with wool or silk, it is still used for overhangings for mantels, borders for table covers and curtains and for furniture coverings. But the modern use of Berlin work has necessitated some modifications in the method of working. Several of the stitches used exclusively in the manufacture of Berlin work are admirably adapted for use on plain and checkered fabrics, namely cross stitch, tent stitch and a combination of the two, also satin and long cross. Perhaps the most popular form of this work is that wrought out with simple cross stitch on checkered or square-meshed fabrics, such as Bargarren art cloth, huck-a-buck, Devonshire art cloth, checkered lawns, scrim and gingham."

Raised work lamp mat with detached fruits made of Berlin wool. The center is worked in cross stitch, c. mid-19th century.

When "ancient" Berlin work was done for furniture coverings, Miss Heron recommended that "dull, dead shades" be used for the design and black or brown for the background. Her book, incidentally, was dedicated to Mrs. Potter Palmer of Chicago, who was greatly interested in textiles and embroidery.

In the needlework advertisements and catalogues, the main interest was in kits for doilies in white and colored silks and cottons, pillows with witty sayings printed on them and collar and cuff sets to be worked in white work and lace. Canvas was available by the yard, both penelope and Berlin, or, as it was sometimes called, colbert canvas. A more expensive one-thread canvas was called antique linen.

Needlepoint canvases were stenciled in this country before the First World War. One such factory was on lower Broadway in the vicinity of the Flatiron Building in New York, and was owned by Mr. Sam Weil. A different stencil was cut for each color used in a design. The stencil was laid on the canvas, which was penelope, the color was painted through the cut out areas and so on through a stack of one hundred or more canvases. Then the next color stencil was lined up on the canvas and the whole process was repeated for that color. This factory was still in operation in the late 1930's but by then the style in needlepoint had changed to "F.I.B.", that is, fill in the background. The "executive part" of the canvas was worked by nimble European or Chinese fingers and the purchaser needed only to fill in the background. Department store needlework departments bought these canvases in great quantities and a generation of American women grew up thinking that this was all there was to needlepoint.

This is not to say that "real" needlepoint was not being done at all. Major cities still had their woman's exchanges, and embroidery shops where canvas and wool could be purchased for original and custom designs. Ladies who could afford it bought beautiful canvases and wool in England, France and Austria.

After World War Two Americans with more leisure time on their

A tiny sampler showing most of the diagrammed stitches. This illustration is almost the actual size of the sampler, one can thus see the relative size of the stitches.

hands took a new look at needlepoint and the current renascence started. The Paternayan Brothers of New York, suppliers of much of the wool used in needlepoint today, were ready with their Persian wool to meet the demand for a long fibred wool with the proper

tent st.	Gobelin (slanting Gobelin)	Irish	German (mosaic)	Mrs. Pullan's version	Raised wool
cross st.				plush st.	
				Turkey work	

flower st.	velvet st.				
	reverse eyelet st.	fancy cross st.	point Russe st.	woven cross st.	woven cross square st.

tied down cross st.	slanting cross st.
	long cross st.
	closed cat st.

triple cross st.	check st.	diagonal knit st.	laced chain st.

Pointe de Tresse st.	vertical tramé st.

Key to sampler

sheen in a wide range of colors. They originally introduced Persian wool to the market in the 1930's. The Paternayan brothers arrived in the United States in 1923 and got their start in the needlework wool business by dying wools with which they repaired antique Aubusson and Persian rugs. Word got around and soon friends in the business were asking for their help and wool. Finding that they were giving too much wool away, they began to sell it and color by color have expanded their line to the more than 400 shades they have today.

It is hoped that this history has widened the horizon of the reader both in doing needlepoint and in understanding needlepoint of the past. Let it never be said that needlepoint is boring; as we have seen, it doesn't have to be!

Drawn work and tapestry sampler worked on five mesh to the inch canvas. The top row is woven bar stitch. The rectangular design is woven on the warp canvas threads. The square window was achieved by weaving the canvas threads back into the canvas. The girl design was also woven on warp canvas threads.

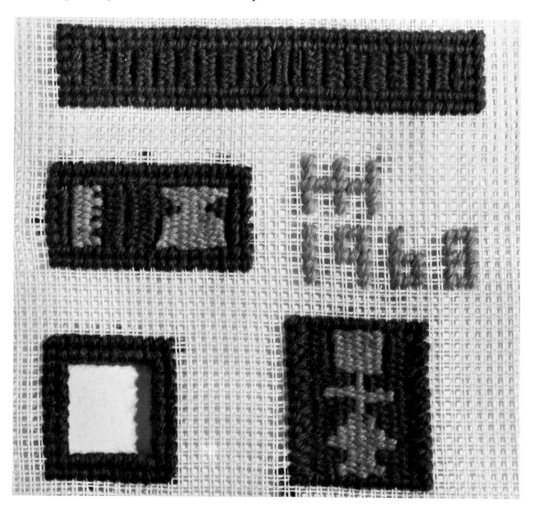

APPENDICES

BIBLIOGRAPHY

PICTURE SOURCES

INDEX

APPENDIX I

THE following is a list of canvases, their use and the approximate date of their introduction to the market. Numbers refer to sources listed on page 149.

BORDER CANVAS
    (1)
From 7 to 18 inches wide
1850's

JAVA CANVAS
    (1)
rug canvas, the threads were woven in pairs, came in various mesh and colors.

RAILWAY CANVAS
a cheap and coarse canvas, came in claret, brown and drab. One kind was made just for use with orné embroidery.

BRACE CANVAS
different from border canvas in that it was silk. Sometimes had a fancy edging; used for suspenders.

IMITATION SILK
CANVAS
the price of silk canvas made the creation of an imitation inevitable.

GENEVA CANVAS
a brown open-meshed bagging on which chenille or worsted was used. Used for tidies and antimasscars. $2.00 in 1874
1874

VICTORIAN CANVAS (3)	black cane bars were couched or inter-woven about every 12 mesh across the weft of the canvas. Grounding could be left bare.	1874
SILVER JARDINIÈRE (3)	canvas could be cut and worked right to the edge. Might have been a form of screening, though it was two-thread.	1875
BURLAP CANVAS (2)	finer mesh than rug canvas, though coarse enough to use double Berlin wool.	1877
JAVA CANVAS (2)	used for Berlin work, no grounding necessary, closely woven mesh like monk's cloth. Around 1888 it was available in wool.	1877
PANAMA CANVAS (2)	a stiff canvas, could be used for straw work, floss or Berlin wool. Needed no grounding.	1877
NET CANVAS (2)	another stiff canvas that came in black and white. Double Zephyr used.	1877
IDA CANVAS (3)	an extra thread was somehow woven into canvas that made a star pattern.	1877
DOUBLE ZEPHYR CANVAS	used for rugs.	1878
BAMBOO CANVAS	quite stiff, ecru in color.	1878
CANVAS GRENADINE	a border canvas, could be used on clothing.	1880
AIDA CANVAS	a coarse linen canvas.	1882
SMYRNA CANVAS	worked with smyrna or leviathan wool, perhaps the same as the rug canvas of today.	1884

TINSEL CANVAS	a metal thread was interwoven. made of jute in olive and black.	1886
RIBBON CANVAS	narrow canvas of fine quality.	1889
CONGRESS CANVAS	cream white in color, with a four-thread locked mesh, sometimes called grenadine too.	1890
CANVAS ANTIQUE	ecru undivided canvas with an interwoven tinsel thread.	1890
TOILE COLBERT	fine meshed undivided cream-colored canvas.	1892
WIRE-TWIST ETAMINE (3)	cotton canvas made of a tightly twisted thread. 5 or 6 inches in width, picoted edges.	1893

1. Mrs. Pullan's *The Lady's Manual of Fancy Work*
2. *Harper's Bazar* from 1874 to 1893
3. S. Annie Frost's *The Ladies' Guide to Needle Work, Embroidery, etc.*

APPENDIX II

CANVAS numbers and mesh corresponding, as shown in Mrs. George Curling Hope's *My Working Friend,* 1851, printed in England.

ENGLISH CANVAS

no. of canvas	16	18	20	22	24	26	on up to	50	55	60	65
mesh to inch		9	10	11	12	13	14		28	30	34	36

FRENCH CANVAS

no. of canvas	10	12	14	16	18	19	20	22	24	26	30	36	40
mesh to inch	13	15	17	19	20	21	22	24	26	28	30	34	36

SILK CANVAS   coarse 21 mesh per inch
                    middle 28 mesh per inch
                    mosaic 40 mesh per inch

APPENDIX III

CANVAS numbers and mesh corresponding, for French cotton canvas, as shown in Mrs. Matilda Pullan's *The Lady's Manual of Fancy Work,* 1857, printed in the United States. Applies to both common and penelope canvas.

no. of canvas	8	10	12	14	16	18	19	20	22	24	30	40	50
mesh to inch	5	6	7	8	9	10	11	12	14	14	15	$16\frac{1}{2}$	18

BIBLIOGRAPHY

EMBROIDERY

AIGUILLETTE (MRS. MATILDA PULLAN), *The Ladies Keepsake, or Treasures of the Needle,* London: Darton and Company, 1851

ASHTON, SIR LEIGH, *Samplers,* London: The Medici Society, 1926

BOLTON, ETHEL STANWOOD and COE, EVA JOHNSTON, *American Samplers,* Boston: Thomas Todd Printers for the Massachusetts Society of the Colonial Dames of America, 1921

COLBY, AVERIL, *Samplers,* Massachusetts: Charles T. Branford Company, 1964

DIGBY, GEORGE WINGFIELD, *Elizabethan Embroidery,* New York: Thomas Yoseloff, 1963

ENTHOVEN, JAQUELINE, *The Stitches of Creative Embroidery,* New York: Reinhold, 1964

FROST, S. ANNIE, *The Ladies' Guide to Needle Work, Embroidery, etc.,* New York; Adam & Bishop, 1877

GROVES, SYLVIA, *The History of Needlework Tools and Accessories,* London: Country Life Limited, 1966

HARTLEY, FLORENCE, *The Ladies' Hand Book of Fancy and Ornamental Work,* Philadelphia, G. G. Evans, 1859

HERON, ADDIE E., *Fancy Work for Pleasure and Profit,* Chicago: Thompson & Thomas, 1905

HOPE, G. CURLING (MRS. GEORGE HOPE), *My Working Friend, Being Plain Directions for the Various Stitches in Fancy Needlework,* England: I. Hope, circa 1851

HUGHES, THERLE, *English Domestic Needlework* 1660–1860, New York, Macmillan, 1961

KENDRICK, A. F., *English Embroidery,* London: G. Newnes Ltd., 1905

LAMBERT, MISS, *The Hand-book of Needlework,* New York: Wiley & Putnam 1842

LENT, D. GENEVA, *Needlepoint as a Hobby,* New York, Harpers, 1942

LESLIE, FRANK, *Frank Leslie's Portfolio of Fancy Needlework,* New York: 1854

MATHEWS, SIBYL I., *Needle-made Rugs,* London: Mills & Boon Ltd., 1963

MAYORCAS, M. J., *English Needlework Carpets, 16th to 19th Centuries,* England, F. Lewis, Ltd., 1963

MORRIS, BARBARA, *Victorian Embroidery,* London, Herbert Jenkins, 1962

OWEN, MRS. HENRY, *The Illuminated Book of Needlework,* London: Henry G. Bohn, 1847

PULLAN, MRS. MATILDA, *The Lady's Manual of Fancy Work,* New York: Dick & Fitzgerald, 1859

REMINGTON, PRESTON, *English Domestic Needlework of the XVI, XVII, XVIII Centuries,* New York: Metropolitan Museum of Art, 1945

SAWARD, BLANCHE, AND CAULFEILD, S. F. A., *The Dictionary of Needlework,* London: A. W. Cowan, 1888

SELIGMAN, G. SAVILLE AND HUGHES, TALBOT, *Domestic Needlework,* London: Country Life, 1926

SYMONDS, MARY (MRS. GUY ANTROBUS) and PREECE, LOUISA, *Needlework Through the Ages,* London: Hodder & Stoughton, Ltd., 1928

THOMAS, MARY, *Mary Thomas's Dictionary of Embroidery Stitches,* London: Hodder & Stoughton, Ltd., 1934

TOWNSEND, W. G. PAULSON, *The Craft of the Needle,* London: Truslove, Hanson & Comba, 1899

WHEELER, CANDACE THURBER, *Development of Embroidery in America,* New York: Harper and Brothers, 1921

WHITING, GERTRUDE, *Tools and Toys of Stitchery,* New York: Columbia University Press, 1928

WILSON, ERICA, *Crewel Embroidery,* New York: Charles Scribner's Sons, 1963

WILTON, COUNTESS OF, *The Art of Needle-work,* London: Henry Colburn, 1844

Ladies' Work for Pleasure and Profit, (anonymous) Chicago: The Home Manual Company, 1894

The Lady's Pocket Companion and Indispensable Friend, (anonymous), New York: Leavitt and Allan, circa 1850

PATTERN BOOKS

FÜRST, ROSINA HELENA, *Neues Model-buch, Vierdter Thiel . . . ,* Nuremberg: Weigel, 1728

GERARDE, JOHN, *The Herball or General Historie of Plantes,* London: Adam Islip, Joice Norton, and Richard Whitakers, 1636

HOFFMAN, WILHELM, *Neues Modelbuch,* 1604, Berlin, Ernst Wasmuth, 1891

LOTZ, ARTHUR, *Bibliographie der Modelbucher,* Stuttgart: Anton Hiersemann, 1963

MOUFET, THOMAS, (MOFFET), *Insectorum,* London: 1634

NETTO, JOHAN FRIEDRICH, *L'Art de Tricoter,* Leipzig: Chez Voss et Compagnie, 1802

NETTO, JOHAN FRIEDRICH, *Taschenbuch der Strick-Stick-Nähund Anderer,* Leipzig: J. C. Hinrichs, 1808

PHILIPSON, A., *Muster von Verschiedenen Blumen, Bouquets, Guirlanden. . . .* , Berlin: J. W. Schmidt, 1803

QUENTEL, PETER, *Musterbuch für Ornamente und Stickmuster von Peter Quentel (1527–1529)*, Facsimile, Leipzig: E. Schloemp, 1882

TOPSELL, EDWARD, *The Historie of Foure-Footed Beastes and Serpents,* London: 1607

VAN MEERTEN, A. B., *Penelope of Maandwerk aan het Vrou-Welijk Geslacht Toegewijd . . . ,* Amsterdam: G. J. A. Beijerinck, 1821–1826

VAVASSORE, GIOVANNI, *Esemplario Di Lavori,* Venice: 1543

WEIGEL, CHRISTOPH, JR., *Des Neues Strick Büchlein,* Nurnberg: 1784

WHITNEY, GEFFREY, *A Choice of Emblemes and Other Devises,* Leyden: 1586

Erstes Toiletten Geschenk Ein Jahrbuch für Damen, Leipzig: Georg Vos, 1805

Zweites Toiletten Geschenk Ein Jahrbuch für Damen, Leipzig, Georg Vos, 1806

Drittes Toiletten Geschenk Ein Jahrbuch für Damen, Leipzig, Georg Vos, 1807

Viertes Toiletten Geschenk Ein Jahrbuch für Damen, Leipzig, Georg Vos, 1808

Muster zum Sticken für Damen, Ausburg: Martin Engelbrecht, 1824

Zeichen-Mahler-und Stickbuch zur Sebstbelchrung für Damen, Leipzig: bei Voss und Compagnie, 1798

FURNITURE

COMSTOCK, HELEN, *American Furniture, 17th, 18th & 19th Century Styles,* New York: The Viking Press, 1962

JOY, EDWARD T., *The Country Life Book of English Furniture,* London: Country Life Ltd., 1964

KOVEL, RALPH AND TERRY, *American Country Furniture 1780–1875,* New York, Crown, 1965

NICKERSON, DAVID, *English Furniture of the Eighteenth Century,* New York, G. P. Putnam, 1963

OTTO, CELIA JACKSON, *American Furniture of the Nineteenth Century,* New York: The Viking Press, 1965

SOUCHAL, GENEVIEVE, *French Eighteenth Century Furniture,* translated by Taylor, Simon Watson, New York: G. P. Putnam's Sons

SWEENEY, JOHN A. H., *Winterthur Illustrated,* A Winterthur Book, 1963

VERLET, PIERRE, *The Eighteenth Century in France, Society, Decoration, Furniture,* Vermont: Charles E. Tuttle Co., 1967

WINCHESTER, ALICE, *Living with Antiques,* New York, E. P. Dutton, 1963

GENERAL

BARNETT, EDWARD BARRY, *Coal Tar Dyes and Intermediates,* London: Bailliere, Tindall & Cox, 1919

BEARD, CHARLES A. AND MARY R., *New Basic History of the United States,* New York, Doubleday, 1960

BISHOP, J. LEANDER, *A History of American Manufactures from 1608 to 1860,* Philadelphia: Edward Young and Company, 1866

BRIDENBAUGH, CARL, *The Colonial Craftsman,* Chicago: Univ. of Chicago Press, 1950

BUNT, CYRIL G. E., *Tudor and Stuart Fabrics,* England: F. Lewis, Ltd., 1961

CLARK, VICTOR S., *History of Manufacturers in the United States, 1607–1860,* reprinted with the permission of the Carnegie Institution of Washington by Peter Smith, New York, 1949

COLE, ANN KILBORN, *The Golden Guide to American Antiques,* New York, Golden Press

DARBY, W. D., *Silk the Queen of Fabrics,* New York: Dry Goods Economist, 1922

DAVIDSON, MARSHALL, (editor) *The American Heritage History of Colonial Antiques,* American Heritage Publishing Company, 1967

DOW, GEORGE FRANCIS, *Arts and Crafts in New England,* 1704–1775, Topsfield, Massachusetts: The Wayside Press, 1927

EARLE, ALICE MORSE, *Child Life in Colonial Days,* New York: Macmillan Company, 1899

JONES, MARY EIRWEN, *British and American Tapestries,* England: Tower Bridge Publications, Ltd., 1952

KLEIN, FREDERIC SHRIVER, *Old Lancaster,* Lancaster, Pennsylvania: Early American Series, 1964

LABARTHE, JULES, *Textiles: Origins to Usage,* New York: Macmillan Company, 1964

LATHROP, ELISE, *Historic Houses of Early America,* New York: Tudor Publishing Company, 1927

LICHTEN, FRANCES, *Decorative Art of Victoria's Era,* New York: Charles Scribner's Sons, 1950

LOVE, THOMAS, *The Art of Dyeing, Cleaning and Scouring and Finishing,* Philadelphia: Henry Carey Baird, 1869

McCLELLAN, ELIZABETH, *History of American Costume,* 1607–1870, New York: Tudor Park, 1937

McCLINTON, KATHARINE M., *The Complete Book of Small Antique Collecting,* New York, Coward-McCann, 1965

PLENDERLEITH, H. J., *The Conservation of Antiquities and Works of Art,* London: Oxford University Press, 1956

SEVENSMA, W. S., *Tapestries,* New York: Universe Books, Inc., 1965 (translated from the Dutch by Brown, Alexis)

THIEME, ULRICH AND BECKER, FELIX, *Allemeines Lexikon der Bildenden Kunstler von der Antike bis zur Gegenwart,* Leipzig: E. A. Seeman, 1930

WARWICK, EDWARD and PITZ, HENRY C., and WYCKOFF, ALEXANDER, *Early American Dress,* New York: Benjamin Blom, 1965

WERTENBAKER, THOMAS JEFFERSON, *A History of American Life,* Vol. II, *The First Americans,* 1607–1690, New York: Macmillan Company, 1927

WERTENBAKER, THOMAS JEFFERSON, *The Old South,* New York: Cooper Square Publishers, 1963

YATES, RAYMOND and MARGUERITE W., *Early American Crafts and Hobbies,* New York: Wilfred Funk, 1954

The American Heritage History of the Thirteen Colonies, American Heritage Publishing Company, 1967

Perkin Centenary London, 100 Years of Synthetic Dyestuffs, New York, Pergamon Press, 1958

CATALOGS AND PAMPHLETS

Fifty Masterpieces of Textiles, London: Victoria and Albert Museum, 1951

Stitches in Time, an Exhibition of Embroideries and Needlework Techniques, New York: The Cooper Union Museum for the Arts of Decoration, 1947

MAGAZINE ARTICLES AND MAGAZINES

BAILEY, WORTH, *Accent on Washingtoniana:* The Yale-de Lancey-Kountze Collection at Mount Vernon, *Antiques* Magazine, 1946

SICKELS, ELIZABETH GALBRAITH, *Thimblemakers in America, Antiques* Magazine, September 1967

Godey's Lady's Book, Philadelphia, 1830 to 1850, 1852, 1858 and 1866, Sarah Hale, Editor

Harper's Bazar, New York, 1869 to 1900 (*Bazar* spelt with one *a* during this period)

Ladies' American Magazine, Vol. I & II, New York: Henry White, 1859

Peterson's Magazine, Philadelphia: 1851, 1855, 1858 to 1861, 1863, 1864, 1867, 1868, 1870 to 1874, 1878, 1881, 1883, 1887, 1888

NEWSPAPERS

The Boston Gazette, and Weekly Republican Journal, Boston, 1719

The Boston News-Letter, and the New England Chronicle, Boston: 1704 to 1735 (This paper changed hands frequently from 1704 to 1763, the title changed almost as often; it was sometimes a weekly, sometimes a semi-weekly.)

Charleston City Gazette and Daily Advertiser, Charleston, South Carolina: 1798

Dunlap's Pennsylvania Packet or the General Advertiser, Philadelphia, 1774

Providence Gazette, Providence, Rhode Island, 1782

Providence Journal, Providence, Rhode Island, 1800

The Virginia Gazette, Williamsburg, Virginia, 1738, 1746, 1751, 1752, 1766 to 1773, 1775 to 1780

PICTURE SOURCES

IN BLACK AND WHITE

THE YALE UNIVERSITY ART GALLERY, The Mabel Brady Garvan Collection, New Haven, Connecticut: page 59 (top right)

THE HENRY FRANCIS DU PONT WINTERTHUR MUSEUM, Wilmington, Delaware: pages 48 (left), 58, 59 (left), 62, 63 (top right, Helga Studio photo), 99 (center)

THE FOLGER SHAKESPEARE LIBRARY, Washington, D.C.: pages 16, 17

THE LIBRARY OF CONGRESS, Washington, D.C.: pages 18, 19

THE NATIONAL TRUST FOR HISTORIC PRESERVATION, Washington, D.C.: page 102 (photo The New York Times)

THE SMITHSONIAN INSTITUTION, Washington, D.C.: pages 47 (top, photo Henry Alexander), 68, 70, 71 (left), 76, 96

THE BOSTON PUBLIC LIBRARY, Boston, Massachusetts: page 57 (George M. Cushing photo) #

THE PILGRIM SOCIETY, Plymouth, Massachusetts: page 35 (right)

THE SOCIETY FOR THE PRESERVATION OF NEW ENGLAND ANTIQUITIES, Boston, Massachusetts: pages 42, 43, 56 #, 63 (top left), 71 (right); photos Richard Merrill

THE BROOKLYN MUSEUM, Brooklyn, New York: pages 23, 29, 32 (left: gift of Frank L. Babbott; right; purchase Henry N. Healy Fund from the collection of Mrs. Grey Antrobus), 77, 83 (top left), 94 (left)

THE COOPER-HEWITT MUSEUM OF DESIGN, New York: page 25

THE METROPOLITAN MUSEUM OF ART, New York: pages 10 (Fletcher Fund, 1927), 13 (Rogers Fund, 1910), 14 (Gift of George R. Hann, 1960), 21 (Rogers Fund, 1929), 26 (Gift of Mrs. Thomas J. Watson, 1939)

THE MUSEUM OF THE CITY OF NEW YORK: pages 41, 61, 74, 75, 80, 103 (and title page), 104, 105 (left)

THE CHESTER COUNTY HISTORICAL SOCIETY, West Chester, Pennsylvania: pages 63 (bottom), 64, 83 (bottom), 87, 108; photos Melvin Gurtizen

THE RED BRICK HOUSE, Middleburg, Virginia: page 49 (right); Del Ankers photo

THE JOHN MARSHALL HOUSE, Richmond, Virginia: page 78; photo Wirt A. Christian, Jr.

THE VALENTINE MUSEUM COLLECTION, Richmond, Virginia: pages 48 (right), 86, 88

COLONIAL WILLIAMSBURG, Williamsburg, Virginia: pages 59 (lower right), 60, 79, 99 (top)

COURTESY OF Miss Katherine Cummings: page 132

COURTESY OF Ginsburg and Levy, New York: page 22

COURTESY OF Mrs. Benjamin Ginsburg: page 105 (left)

COURTESY OF Miss Elinor M. Parker: page 138 (top); photo Henry Alexander. The rug was worked in the 1870's for her mother's dolls' house by her grandmother, Mrs. George Fuller.

COURTESY OF Miss Elizabeth M. Riley: pages 52, 99 (bottom)

COURTESY OF Mrs. Doris Thompson: page 19 (bottom)

FROM THE AUTHOR'S COLLECTION: pages 28, 35 (left), 41 (left), 45, 47 (bottom left and right), 49 (left), 67, 72, 83 (top right), 89*, 91, 92, 93, 94 (right), 100, 111, 119, 128, 131*, 137, 138 (bottom)*, 139*, 142*, 144*

*photos Henry Alexander

reprinted by permission of *Antiques* magazine from an article by Nancy Graves Cabot, December 1950

IN COLOR

FRONTISPIECE, Courtesy of Ginsburg and Levy, New York, photo Helga Studio

FACING PAGE 30. Colonial Williamsburg

FACING PAGES 38, 84 (upper right), 98, 140. The Smithsonian Institution

FACING PAGE 84 (bottom). Chester County Historical Society

FACING PAGE 84 (upper right). The author, photo Henry Alexander

INDEX